ACPL IT Y0-BYU-046

DISCARDED

5-23-67

Technical Assistance—
Theory and
Guidelines

Technical Assistance–
Theory and
Guidelines

SIDNEY C. SUFRIN

SYRACUSE UNIVERSITY PRESS

Copyright © 1966
By Syracuse University Press
Syracuse, New York

ALL RIGHTS RESERVED

First Edition 1966

Library of Congress
Catalog Card: 66-29623

Manufactured in the
United States of America

To A. AND A., V. AND S.
Who Stood by When the Going Was Rough

1410876

Introduction
and Acknowledgments

The purpose of this book is to examine some of the administrative problems associated with technical assistance to underdeveloped countries by technically advanced nations. The study is not directly concerned with any of the social disciplines—anthropology, economics, sociology, or political science. The emphasis, rather, is on the technical assistance process, which like any other social process provides the experimental, or at least factual, base for analysis and concept creation, which in turn leads to theorizing. The social scientist, therefore, as a member of a discipline, is not likely to gain knowledge of his particular field of study by reading this book. By use of an inter-disciplinary approach, I hope to aid in placing the complex social process of technical assistance into meaningful perspective.

In any discussion of technical assistance, it is important to realize that the donor country is not a free agent. The attitudes, values, and political climate of the host country limit the choices of the donor. International political situations must also be considered; competition exists among actual and potential donors. The Soviet Union competes with the United States, or even with Soviet China. But competition exists among the friendlier powers also, as we shall see. France, Britain, and other nations "want in" and are willing to adjust their programs to assure acceptance. Assistance can only be measured against what the politics of the situation allow.

Furthermore, a program designed to strengthen a given developing society, an Arab state for example, has inevitable repercussions on the donor's relations with other states, Israel, in this example. The flow of repercussions may be in two directions. Within the United States, too, the various agencies concerned with the implementation of assistance may not have the same interests, or they may not agree concerning the appropriateness of specialized assistance. The Department of Agriculture does not see the issues in the same way, e.g., that the State Department sees them. The possibilities of justifiable alternative policies and programs are numerous and diverse.

Technical assistance is an aspect of cultural diffusion in that the problem is the transference or origination, by means of advice, of new ways of social behavior. The successful program transfers or originates economic and other social techniques which raise the standard of living of the host country. To be sure, technical assistance rarely produces self-contained or well-defined institutional changes. Rather, change in one area tends to proliferate and spread to other processes. As underdeveloped societies undergo change because of contacts with trade and ideas of the rest of the world, however, the ensuing development (change) makes possible what one might consider the localization of additional change. That is, a society with a public budget, an air-transport industry, or a banking system, often finds that changes in such institutions are limited to those institutions, and they neither produce nor require broader changes. This, in part, is an argument of this book.

The basic data for discussion was secured from source material of the Agency for International Development (AID), but without access to any secret or confidential files. The data, though generally not available, was either unclassified or classified as "restricted." Another source upon which I drew, although not always in a specific sense, was the work of Talcott Parsons, and Parsons and Smelser in their conception of formal institutional change. Their writings (which I used for both specific references and general background) forced my thoughts into the mold which this work finally took.

This study presupposes the importance of agriculture in most developing societies. The major short-range problem is to feed more people more adequately than is being done by existing organization and resources.

Technical assistance is the diffusion of ideas from a technically rich society to a technically poorer society. The great discussion of cultural interplay has been a special province of the anthropologists. Therefore, the work starts with a brief *aperçu* of what some anthropologists have written on cultural diffusion (Chapter I). From the reflective, general view, we next move to what practitioners have said about technical assistance from the aspect of idea transference. This discussion is based on the reports of assistance officers of AID, and a number of selected case studies. Again because of the special role of agriculture, the findings in that area are segregated. It is interesting to note that while the academic reflections and experiences reported in Chapter I often deal with interrelations and implications of given technical innovations, the sense of the interconnectedness of innovation is not very well marked in the reports and cases of the practitioners (AID officials). Yet the essence of technical diffusion is that a change, once introduced, *may* spread to other phases of social life (Chapters II, III, and IV).

This linkage or quality of interconnectedness of technical assistance is discussed in Chapter V, with special reference to agriculture. The AID study, of which the original work of this book was a part, was concerned with agriculture. But of even greater interest is the probability that the low development of agriculture makes the need and concern with interrelations of technical assistance more obvious there than for industry or trade. Furthermore, the probable high degree of economic rationality in agriculture implies that other forms of economic activity, based more nearly on Western modalities and values, are more rational than is often asserted. Thus, while the practitioner must of necessity focus on the immediate problems at hand, the planners must always consider the time and repercussion dimensions of technical assistance, while recognizing that economic rationality itself is dependent on the setting of the problem.

This book, in part, is my contribution to a large study conducted under a grant to Syracuse University from AID on the administration of technical assistance. Later work was done under a grant from the Inter-University Institution Building Program sponsored by the universities of Indiana, Pittsburgh, Michigan State, and Syracuse.

My thanks are due to these universities, John Lindeman, AID project director, and Irving Swerdlow, associate dean of the Maxwell School of Syracuse University. Both men have shown a kindness and patience not always consonant with administrative timetables. I should also like to thank Tariq Siddiqui, of Pakistan, Arun Shourie, of India, and Morton Stelcner, of Canada, who assisted me. Dr. Siddiqui's insights were especially helpful. John Huber, of the Department of State, S. M. Miller, of New York University, Julian Friedman, Timothy Rice, and Gordon Bowles, of Syracuse University, read the manuscript in various phases of development and suggested additions and deletions. To them my gratitude is great indeed.

The draft typing was done by Mrs. Anne Rath and Mrs. Virginia Halsey, the greater burden of which was carried by Mrs. Halsey. The good sense and instinct of workmanship of these ladies beggar my ability to thank them. Mrs. Thelma Clark typed the final copy of the manuscript with her usual dispatch.

The argument, however, and the errors of omission and commission are, as is always the case, my personal responsibility.

August 4, 1966
Syracuse, New York

SIDNEY C. SUFRIN

Contents

Technical Assistance—
Theory and
Guidelines

I. A Reflection on Cultural Diffusion

Societies which are in contact with each other through trade, tourism (which in itself is a kind of international trade), political arrangements, technical assistance, military cooperation or conflict, indeed nearly any type of cultural propinquity, tend to exchange some artistic, organizational, technical, and even ideological characteristics and traits. The American Indian, for example, taught the white settlers how to fight in the forest; but on the other hand, the white settlers taught the Indians how to use firearms. Similarly, alcoholic spirits were an exchange for corn and jerked meat. Social contacts tend to be transactions in the ordinary sense of that word.

In the present day the Western World's political and economic concern with poorer, underdeveloped countries is indicated by the popularity of Asian and African art objects in many American and European homes. The subject matter of popular novels, television programs, and motion pictures, as well as clothing styles and light amusements, e.g., dances, sometimes derive, in one way or another, from the less-developed world. Another aspect of mutual exchange is that some vague conception of Western European democratic socialism and party dictatorship, *inter alia,* has virtually permeated the technologically underdeveloped world, as if in exchange for the Western borrowings.[1]

While political protest in the Colonial world is as old as the Colonial world itself, it was not until the period after World War II that freedom and independence for most of Africa and Asia became a potential reality instead of a revolutionary dream. Even

[1] J. Viner, "The U.S. as a Welfare State," *The Nation's Economic Objectives,* ed. by E. O. Edwards (Chicago: University of Chicago Press, 1964), p. 161.

1

South American revolutionary ideology acquired more mass support and pragmatic orientation after the war. Some idea of "socialism" or mass involvement in the benefits of the society is an almost universal ideal in the developing world. This, it may be argued, is an adaptation of the ideology of Western Europe which has so thoroughly infused world political, literary, and social thought in the late nineteenth and early twentieth centuries.

The underdeveloped world, when it was still bound by the colonial ideology prior to 1940, made great use of the technology of the West. But after independence, some aspects of Western organizational forms (e.g., land tenure and social insurance) were often adapted to the particular needs and purposes conceived by the leadership of the developing nation in question.

A significant result of the growing importance of the poorer nations (by Western social standards) has been the changed role of the colored peoples in the thinking of the West, and of white people in general. It is far too simple to ascribe the concern of the West entirely to keeping the underdeveloped world from falling into the Communist camp or the Communist way of thinking. It is probable that even without the threat of Communism, the West—after the great cataclysm of a World War—would have directed its attention to the underdeveloped world partly out of a sincere desire to secure international stability through social improvement. "Improvement" in this context means a rising standard of living, some conceptions of social justice, and a tolerably smooth set of international relations.

Furthermore, World War II exposed an essential instability and confusion in the white world. Not only did the white world get itself into the impossible predicament, i.e., Western white man's world war plus military setbacks by the Japanese, but less-developed nations were courted for their manpower, resources, location, and general political favor. Promises of freedom, increased income, and preferential treatment were part of the gifts brought by the warring West to the underdeveloped world in return for its support or at least for its neutrality. After the war, political uncertainties and upsurges required that the promises be paid, either willingly or under protest. Freedom and independence are only part of the payment.

RECIPROCATION IN PRACTICE

In a mutual exchange, the country which is the recipient of those technologies, ideologies, or organizational ideas which induce significant social change may be deemed the "less-developed" or "poorer." Conversely, the country which receives technologies, ideologies, or organizational ideas which have relatively little effect on the way of life of the country may be deemed to be "more developed" or richer. This distinction does not hold equally if one considers the exchange of goods. The underdeveloped world is often the supplier of primary products—raw materials such as ores, oil, timber, and some agricultural products. Such products are often essential to the life and operation of developed societies. Great Britain, Western Europe generally, Japan, and the United States are not, in any operational sense, economically self-sufficient at their present levels of consumption; nor would their mutual trade, *inter se,* be possible at existing levels and composition without the contributions of the less well-developed trading partners. This is in part, despite the fact that the terms of trade are probably moving against the poorer countries, the result of their growing reliance on the products of the developed countries.

The postwar noneconomic imports of the West from the underdeveloped world have, on the whole, been trivial—trivial in the sense that such imports have not vitally affected the life and the organization of the West. Artistic forms in written and cinematic literature, some few musical forms and devices, and possibly the novelty of new places to visit have been the major "imports." Western philosophy, politics, and science have not been significantly enriched. Gandhi's nonviolent philosophy is a signal contribution to pressure politics, but this derives in part from Henry David Thoreau, a New Englander.

The major export to the West from the underdeveloped area has been political—the concern that political and social structures of the underdeveloped world are not functioning smoothly as to provide a rising standard of living and a secure life for the people in the underdeveloped world. This dysfunctioning of society is not only an evil unto itself, but also a threat to the peace and security of the world.

The persistent and increasing divergence of income and well-being between rich and poor countries is a constant source of friction and political or economic trouble. Time is not on the side of those who would slowly work toward the development of the new societies. The tensions between the haves and the have-nots, between the adept and the clumsy, are becoming greater, not less. The efforts of the Western World have not been rewarded by great success in development, in view of the wars, revolutions, and hatreds that have evolved.

A by-product of the Western contacts with the underdeveloped world has been the granting of status and stature to the people of these areas, particularly to individuals: U Thant, Nehru, Gandhi, Nkrumah, Sukarno, Kenyatta, the Diem family—these and many other names have become known to the Western man on the street. Organizations too have become known—the African Liberation Army, the Viet Cong, the Congress party, and Organization of American States—and are mentioned in the public press with almost no explanation needed.

Yet since World War II—more specifically, since the middle of the 1950's—the contacts, borrowings, and lendings between the West and the underdeveloped world have not resulted in a feeling of accomplishment on the part of the West because the underdeveloped world is in a turmoil, politically, economically, and socially. Within this turmoil there is the possibility that some meaningful, successful changes have taken place as a result of the blind pulling and hauling, as well as a result of coordinated efforts and planning on the part of the West and the changing societies. Order may emerge, and what seems to be turmoil may be the process of social ordering.

The Complexity of Development

When in the middle of the 1950's the Western world, particularly the United States with its Point Four program, accepted the improvement of the underdeveloped world as a matter of vital policy, economists found or believed they had found, the great cause for the economic backwardness of the poor countries in the scarcity of capital. As the analysis grew more sophisticated, however, and as more disciplines were involved in analyzing the problems of economic growth, it became clear that economic development is but one element in social change. Other considerations—ideological, organizational, and structural—are all part of the same social fabric. Development (or change) is not usually limited to a single aspect of society. When change occurs it tends to take place in many aspects of living, best seen at the local level.

To the Western mind, development is often measured by the social structures and social accomplishments of the West. This is understandable since the indices of social success with which we are most familiar are the indices which we use to measure our own social success or failure. The nation-states outside Northwestern Europe considered successful by Western European ideologists are, for the most part, former colonies of Western European powers. These neo-European states are heirs to the social, economic, political, and ideological structures of Northwestern Europe. Such states may have changed their heirlooms or modified them to suit the particular and peculiar needs and circumstances of the new societies, but the United States, British Canada, Australia, French Canada, and South Africa are culturally and ideologically Western European societies.

Not all newly developed states pattern themselves to Western standards. Japan, which developed a successful, effective economic structure to supplement its general cultural developments, clearly is not an ethnic child of Northwestern Europe. Israel, on the other hand, certainly drew its people, leadership, and technology from Western Europe, and so is somewhat like a colonial possession which has won independence. Hong Kong, the strange city-state, did develop on a different ethnic base than other high-income societies, and it used the indigenous population, or at least the non-Western population, in its development. In law and technology, Hong Kong derives much from the West. The Arab States, also formerly part of Western Empires, show tendencies which doubtless are related to their previous forced contacts with Western Europe.

It is interesting to observe that the former Western colonial possessions which became great and powerful nation-states did not usually rely to any extent upon the indigenous population. Indeed, in the United States, African Negroes were imported as slaves. Western Europeans planned and controlled the enterprise, however, while the American Indian contributed virtually nothing to American society. In Latin America generally, social success, measured by Western European standards, has not been overwhelmingly great. But on that continent Western culture has been successful (by Western standards) where it has not been heavily diluted by other cultures, and where its cultural borrowings have been fairly discriminating in favor of Western institutions.

This is not to assert that Western culture is the ideal index for measuring all other cultures, or that cultures which do not parallel those of Western Europe are inferior or unsuccessful. It is to assert that the criteria of success used by Western Europeans for other cultures usually tends to be, either consciously or unconsciously, the ideals of Western society.

Yet, subcultures of the Western world such as technological and mercantile proficiency, have been exported, sometimes with great success to the non-Western world. Leaving out Japan, which has had an unrivaled success in nearly all fields of endeavor, it appears that the military subculture has been successfully proliferated from the West to the non-West. But the borrowings of the non-West from the West have, fortunately, not been limited to military matters. For example, hospitals, medical care, the modern arts of medicine and surgery are widespread in the world, and to a great extent reflect the growth of the Americo-European medical subculture. Under some circumstances, then, probably owing in part to the differences in cultural viability, cultural diffusion on a grand or subcultural (institutional) scale occurs more easily and readily in some countries than in others, but in general is not widespread.

Generality and Uniqueness

Broad general questions, such as "Why did one country develop while another did not?" "What are the conditions or circumstances which permit general development?" and "Which circumstances and considerations are detrimental to development?" are extremely complex. They are too large indeed to be answered in any ultimate or definitive way. Too many variables peculiar to particular times and places are found in the process of development—climate, resources, personalities, historical circumstances, social accidents, political considerations at home and abroad, world conditions of employment, and demand for materials. These and others are often autonomous variables in quality and are often unique or at least limited to particular situations.

More subtle variables are the institutional structure of countries and the unique structures of their ideologies and Utopian hopes. When dealing with such broad and often vague considerations one can only argue in terms of rough probabilities that suggest general impressions which might be of help in dealing with specific problems in specific places.

It is, however, the smaller questions which are the more manageable. But their very manageability may turn out to be a snare and a delusion in adducing meaningful generalizations. The introduction of a new tool in a primitive society, a steel ax, for example, has been done with ease and apparently without any special preparation. Yet the substitution of a steel ax for a stone ax, successful in itself in this particular case, produced very slight beneficial results because the natives used the steel ax as they had used the stone ax—only to cut.[2] The other capacities of a steel ax-head—to pound and break—simply were not exploited.

In this case, the introduction of a novel device did not create a significant change in social behavior. On the other hand, the introduction of *Hevea Braziliensis* (the rubber tree) to the East Indies had great effects on the Indonesian economy and culture. Climate, administration, land resources, population, etc., were all involved in the change. Neither Africa nor South America, the home of the tree, reacted similarly.

Minor changes, to be meaningful, must adjust to the social setting. For example, a poor society in which poverty is endemic might be expected to improve its status if, through some system of loans by the government or cooperatives, the immediate fear of starvation could be removed. Yet providing such a peasant community with funds, in and of itself, does not assure that the funds will be used for anything but immediate consumption.[3] The farmers must learn to think ahead for a whole crop year or even for a two-crop cycle, and if funds are to result in capital accumulation, the farmers must plan to improve their stock. The point is that in a Burmese example given in the UNESCO study just cited, the

---

[2] Lauriston Sharp, "Steel Axes for Stone Age Australians," *Human Problems in Technological Change,* ed. by Edward H. Spicer (New York: Russell Sage Foundation, 1952), p. 82.

[3] Margaret Mead (ed.), *Cultural Patterns and Technical Change* (World Federation of Mental Health, UNESCO: Paris, 1953), p. 71.

farmers borrowed money to avoid poverty rather than to create wealth. The notions of economic security and of the complexity of the roundabout system of production do not exist in a society which subsists from crop year to crop year.

Even if a hypothetical peasant community, by main strength and awkwardness, were able to shift its interest from the present to the future, it is dubious if the capital accumulation could be successful without other ancillary changes in the institutional framework. Were there roads to transport the additional products to market, or was other transport available? If there was transport, could farmers finance their expected crops through a credit system? Were there markets to sell the crops, and, of equal importance, were there consumer goods to buy to satisfy the pressing needs of the (hypothetical) peasant community? The mere provision of technology and capital might have actually made a bad situation worse by frustrating the farmers whose expectations were raised in anticipation of the immediate salvation. One might extend this argument and ask if the increased output of agriculture and a concomitant demand for consumer goods might not have upset the foreign trade policy of the government, its investment policy, its price level policy, etc. In other words, an economic innovation which appears trivial at first sight may, in essence, require rather great economic innovations affecting the national economy. The smallness of successful change does not imply triviality, nor is every attempt at change necessarily directed to the basic ideology on institutional structure. Many, perhaps most, innovations require personnel, skill, funds, and resources. They succeed by grafting a new way of behaving to the existing society without being profound in their effects. Attempts at change may be successful or unsuccessful without involving the basic fabric of the society. It is the basic changes which, however, will ultimately convert a poorly developed society to a well-developed one. The ideal type is Japan.

One might go on to argue that just as the macroeconomy of the nation is made up of geographically situated or firmly orientated microeconomies, so the economic system itself is related to the political system, the social system, the artistic system, the religious system, the system of values, and other subcultural systems. In other words, as we view it, each society is an entirety, a fabric, and we must find some loose strings on which to pull if we are to unravel the society for analytical purposes. It is at this point that the economist must look to the anthropologist for assistance.

THE ENLIGHTENING ROLE OF ANTHROPOLOGY

Anthropologists are in general agreement that contacting cultures interact with one another. Culture in this context is defined as a model or abstraction of learned behavior which is transmitted through all the people of the society, including immigrants who become members of the society. Learned behavior is not limited to any particular aspect of human endeavor, but includes arts, sciences, religion and philosophy, technology, political practices, and the details of life which are not peculiar to a particular family but are generally widespread, such as food habits and political techniques or, indeed, any kind of organized behavior.[4] The essence of culture is that it consists of learned behavior, and so is not natural in the sense of being automatic or instinctive.

The central idea of cultural diffusion is the notion that individual and social behavior can be changed, and that given stimuli in the form of aid, advice, payments, examples of technology, organization, etc., will produce behavioral changes. This applies to profound as well as superficial changes. Two points which need to be considered before the formal statement can be put into operation are:

1. What behavior patterns are wanted, and
2. What changes or factors can bring such behavior about.

Desired behavior patterns (1 above) must be made legitimate in some fashion by the members of the affected society and, if accomplished, may require changes in other behavior patterns (institutions). Furthermore, the stimuli (2 above) must also be made legitimate for the society, because means cannot be solely justified by ends but in themselves must have a legitimate base. By legitimation, we mean the sanctioning of a social process according principles accepted by the society. In brief, we may call such principles moral. Legitimation is important because it levies restraints on reform. Genocide or the starvation of a select quota

[4] *Ibid.*, p. 9.

of peasants may work for a time as a solution to the population problem, but it will not be popular, permanent, or acceptable as general policy.

The key issue seems to be the question of how patterns of social behavior are affected in the transmission of cultural ideas, especially in technology, which is our central concern. Are social behavior patterns affected by changes induced into the mechanism or ideology of the institution by individuals, or are they changed by people who, as leaders, induce other individuals to behave in some new fashion? In other words, do institutions interact with other institutions, or do people interact with other people? Bronislaw Malinowski supports the conception of cultural penetration, i.e., institutional reaction.[5]

Malinowski's brief argument is that "units of transformation are not traits or trait complexes but organized systems or institutions."[6] What Malinowski argues, with some of his fellow anthropologists, is that institutions are useful in accomplishing goals, and in a sense this utility gives them a charter or legitimates them. Thus institutions may be seen as means to ends, or as means and ends, but purpose is implicit in the idea of a group habit. Purpose may be trivial or serious, but it is always present. Malinowski finds, for example, that when the European states in the colonial era attempted to introduce "advanced" practices into Africa—practices which included schools, medical services, and Christianity—confusion resulted, because the principle of all people being children of God (taught by Christianity) was frustrating since the operating institutions (schools and hospitals) tended to separate whites from blacks. Institutions could not be successful because their implied techniques—segregation being one of the techniques—frustrated a value or the ideological conception of equality. The result was a series of reactions which had a profound effect upon the ideology and the social structure of the natives, an effect which the whites did not expect.[7]

In Malinowski's view, the introduction of a new set of institu-

---

[5] Bronislaw Malinowski, *The Dynamics of Cultural Change: An Inquiry into Race Relations in Africa,* ed. by Phyllis M. Cabery (New Haven: Yale University Press, 1954).

[6] *Ibid.,* p. 119.

[7] *Ibid.,* p. 57.

tional behavior patterns into the African scene resulted in a chaotic or disorientated society which, if it were to continue in any fashion, had to devise new institutions with new charters and legitimations. The profound changes introduced affected public administration, morality, religion, family structure, etc. In other words, the institutions which served a purpose in Europe when introduced into Africa resulted in frustration and even chaos until a new synthesis evolved.[8] That individuals were carriers of ideas or that they put the ideas into practice, or even administered the arrangements is obvious, because social events require people. Malinowski's contention is that the relevant consideration is not the chance carriers who might very well have been other people than those chosen to carry on the task of changing the institution life of Africa, rather it is the impact of European institutions on African life. To be sure, the introduction of the plow, for example, might have wide effects on output, manpower requirements, the quality of produce, and other matters. The agricultural institutions of the African society might absorb the effects of the plow. In such a case all that has happened is that the individuals who are the receivers of the new technology use it, and in a sense weave the plow-related changes into the existing institutional fabric. But if the changes were great, the agricultural and related institutions would be changed.

Another view, often associated with the name of Professor Radcliffe-Brown, is that interactions such as cultural diffusion depend mainly on the interactions between persons and groups *within* an established structure or institution.[9] Individuals or groups of people transmit new ideas to other individuals or groups, who react by rejecting, accepting, or modifying the ideas. The process of legitimation and the charter of the institution are implied to the observer by the actions of people. Institutions are artifacts of the legitimation process and have no life of their own. Social events occur through the behavior of people, and observed social behavior is always personal. Habits, procedures, values, and goals are learned by people from people.

[8] *Ibid.,* p. 71.
[9] Ian Hogbin, *Social Change* (London: Watts, 1958), p. 22; A. R. Radcliffe-Brown, *Applied Anthropology* (Brisbane: Australian and New Zealand Association for the Advancement of Science, 1930), p. 69.

We have attempted to polarize the two views of social change because each has its often unreflecting proponents among practical people concerned with administering technical assistance. Radcliffe-Brown's views on this subject are that "the transmission of learnt ways of thinking, feeling and acting contribute to the cultural process, which is a specific feature of human life."[10] He goes on to say that "it is, of course, part of that process of interaction amongst persons which is here defined as the social process thought of as the social reality."[11] It is also his view that "the process [of social life] consists of . . . actions and interactions of human beings, acting as individuals or in combinations or groupings."[12] Yet to the interested outsider who is trying to find out something about cultural diffusion in the realm of social change, the two views do not seem to be inconsistent.

As we pointed out above, events in the social sphere are meaningful insofar as they affect human behavior as evidenced ultimately by the actions of individuals. Such words as "meaning," "importance," and "effectiveness" imply that individuals are changed by events. Indeed, one might go so far as to say that events have their meaning *in* individuals.

Whether persons act as a group or as individuals has enormous significance. No one denies the existence and significance of group behavior, especially when formalized into institutional patterns. But even in an institution the unit is the individual who behaves in accordance with the pressures and forces acting upon him. The institution and the individual are firmly related, even symbiotically, if the idea is accepted that an institution can enter into a relation with a person. The result is that institutional behavior is rarely formalized to the point of being without elasticity or the capacity to change. Such elasticity persists because people are flexible and always the subject and object of change.

For our purposes we may ignore the situation in which a person has his mode of life changed by some external idea, provided, of course, that this single person does not seriously affect the institutional behavior of other people. So far as a person (or family)

10 Radcliffe-Brown, *Structure and Function in Primitive Society* (Glencoe, Ill.: Free Press, 1953), p. 5.
11 *Ibid.*, pp. 4–5.
12 Radcliffe-Brown, *op. cit.*

changes food habits or method of prayer, or conception of right or wrong, *without* affecting other people, we may consider the changes entirely trivial. Actions become significant when they affect a group, but the group, we must remember, consists of individuals who behave in some joint, patterned, and ordered fashion which may change to some other joint, patterned, ordered fashion. The crux seems to be the consideration of the circumstances under which joint or ordered (i.e., institutional) purposive behavior differs from that previously followed.

But while the group has no existence other than through the joint action of individuals, the individual tends to learn from the leaders of the group. New institutional behavior patterns usually imply the legitimation of such behavior by some internalized value system on the part of individuals. Behavior must be viewed by individuals as an effective, legitimate means to certain meaningful ends.

How social and individual actions become legitimized, and how a new order is inculcated in a number of people are relevant questions. In many, perhaps the most successful instances, new behavior and its legitimation to social acceptance, must be initially introduced by some individual or group of individuals who have the status and the power to make the new procedure acceptable. That such behavior, which is apparently legitimate under some circumstances, turns out to be not so under others—Malinowski's case of Christianity and segregation being incompatible—is, of course, a lively possibility. On the other hand, the legitimation of hospitals, even though they employ segregation, has occurred without chaos, except perhaps to the associations of witch doctors. If the witch doctors have sufficient power to thwart hospitals and medical care, chaos might very well result in a showdown in which witch doctory would replace Western scientific medicine. If witch doctory turns out to be less effective in the minds of the individuals who are subject to it, then Western scientific medicine will take its place. If Western scientific medicine employs segregation which has lost its legitimation, then it presumably will change, or become the object of criticism. Dr. Albert Schweitzer's hospital has in recent years been criticized because of its "nineteenth-century social structure." Yet the hospital has virtually made Dr. Schweitzer a secular saint by nineteenth-century standards.

In the discussion of social development and cultural diffusion, the persistence of the new institutions is an issue. Let us take a hypothetical case of an African or an Indian village in which small-pox is raging. Field doctors come in to vaccinate or inoculate the villagers. Let us assume further that the equivalent of the medical profession of the village is agreeable to this activity, indeed, urges it. The injections are made, and the villagers are saved. This, in itself, doesn't provide proof that modern medicine is acceptable to the village. As anthropologists have pointed out, a vaccination or injection may have some distant, but nevertheless recognizable, relation to certain rites which include blood letting, so that there is a persistent pattern of behavior of villagers. No cultural diffusion of any significance has occurred. The episode is still on the level of triviality. If, on the other hand, the medical team attempts to follow up its success by changing the practices of midwifery, bone setting or the treatment of tuberculosis, and the villagers accept the new order of things partly on the basis of some of the earlier successful experiences of the medical team, and work to assist in building a hospital, latrines, and change their behavior and expectations, then the new institution of medicine is accepted in the community. That such an innovation will affect other behavior patterns is beyond doubt.

The converse, however, might also be true—that simply because the epidemic was stopped in its tracks, the villagers see no reason to change their habits and procedures. The question is how does one go about "selling" the idea of modern medicine to the village? This implies cultural hurdles.

Professor Bharati defines cultural hurdles as "the traditional attitudes or customs which are part of the cultural base of a particular region and which constitute barriers to innovation."[13] He views such cultural hurdles as institutional, not as innate in national character. In India, for example, Bharati finds that the Indian lives in two worlds. One is the usual phenomenal world of experience; the other is the unworld or anti-world. The former is similar to the typical conceptions of the world outside India, the

[13] Agehananda Bharati, "Cultural Hurdles in Development Administration," *Development Administration: Concepts and Problems,* ed. by Irving Swerdlow (Syracuse: Syracuse University Press, 1963), p. 68.

world of things and institutions, of overt behavior and purposes. The latter—the unworld—is one of ideals, magic, and mystery and is unique to India. Programs of action, then, must somehow be adjusted to the two settings, or if possible, within a reasonable time and with reasonable efforts, the settings themselves might be changed.

In such a society the administrator of a particular project has difficulty in gaining acceptance because his worldly activity often is judged by unworldly criteria, so his job appears irrelevant.[14] The hurdle of culture cannot be jumped because the jumper and the hurdle are not in the same universe of discourse. But there are other reasons why the administrator from the outside is not to be trusted and so cannot overcome the cultural barrier. Villagers have little control over their own lives. Significant decisions are often made by people from the outside. Taxes, restrictions, and wars, to name but three types of institutional intervention, are determined outside the village and are enforced by outsiders. The villager, therefore, sees the outside as "foreign" and its representative not to be trusted.[15] Furthermore, because the village is essentially a static complex of institutions, changes in power and income do not represent accretions of power and income but *redistributions* of these important facets of life, so that if one person is more fortunate, another person tends to be unfortunate.[16] In order to get a certain regulation approved in an Indian village, Bharati cites the case of a holy man who was in accord with a certain regulation toward which the villagers were cool. The priest won his point by citing (nonexistent) Scripture to show that what was wanted by the outside administration was really in accord with and approved by religion.[17] The villagers accepted the legitimation without question.

Here we have a situation in which legitimation of institutional behavior is made by reference to a nonexistent charter, but the legitimation is accepted because an institutional leader points the

[14] *Ibid.*, p. 71.
[15] George M. Foster, *Traditional Culture and the Impact of Technological Change* (New York: Harpers, 1962), p. 47.
[16] *Ibid.*, p. 54.
[17] Bharati, *op. cit.*, pp. 74, 82.

way and creates, arbitrarily, the legitimation. In general, legitimation by custom is more persistent than legitimation by power and force.

The legitimation of a new behavior pattern by fitting it into the values of an existing institution is the lesson to be learned from the anthropological casebook, *Human Problems and Technical Change*.[18] This volume is a series of essays dealing with such varied experiences as the introduction of hybrid corn to an American Indian village, the attempts to dig wells in a Peruvian village, an industrial relations problem in the Caroline Islands, and how fertilizers were introduced to an Indian village. All seem to point out that the successful introduction of technology is related to the use and adaptation of existing institutional forms by indigenous leaders of the institutions. According to these essays, the changes wrought, or frustrated in the attempts, are concerned with technology and not with moral questions. In the successful experiences, however, the morality of the community was not outraged or markedly changed by the technological introduction.

The Operational Approach

It is interesting to consider what would happen if a powerful faction of a society preferred a low standard of living, an attitude which Westerners would consider an untoward ideological value; but also suppose that some of the social leaders, with less than an overwhelming following, desired Westernization or development. In such cases one is inclined to believe that purposive change in the form of organization or technological innovation would be frustrated, unless the essential value system were changed, i.e., a workable value consensus were arrived at by the society and the leaders. The great names of history, the heroes in Sidney Hook's sense,[19] the eventmakers, surely had a role in changing values as the precondition of changing institutional arrangements.

In the developing societies of the world, the moral changes attendant upon creating a new order have occurred or are well under way. The African cry *"Uhuru,"* the anti-imperialism of Asia and India, the upsurge in Latin America, are summed up in the rather

---

[18] Sharp, *op. cit.*

[19] *The Hero in History: A Study in Limitation and Possibility* (New York: John Day, 1943).

vague expression, "the revolution of rising expectations." In a very real sense we are undergoing a revolution against a world in which the masses had no hope, and in which great, purposive change only recently seemed unlikely. Suddenly, after World War II, the underdeveloped world saw freedom, independence, security, and a high standard of living almost within its grasp.

This ideological and moral awakening implies that the institutional structures of emerging societies, the patterned, ordered ways of behavior, are undergoing changes because the purpose, the charter, the legitimation of possible new behavioral forms have emerged. The underdeveloped world cannot be treated as the aboriginal world whose institutions are unrelated to those of the West. The fact that the underdeveloped world is seeking change— "progress and betterment"—is, in essence, the result of the interaction of Western European, Soviet, and indigenous institutions and ideologies. Ideals associated with technology, socialism, communism, democracy, freedom, security, improved living standards, these have become general values in the world, though they are interpreted quite differently in different places and under different circumstances.

The degree to which these (ideologic) values persist is an important determinant in the degree to which the institutional means which are directed toward these values will persist. But persistence does not mean that the patterns of behavior are static and unchanging. A persistent institution is one whose very flexibility permits it to adjust to changing times and circumstances. This is what Radcliffe-Brown meant (in the essay cited above) when he wrote, "social change consists essentially in processes of integration and disintegration." The kinship family structure, for example, tends to break down when it becomes clear to the actors of the social scene that some other family structure is more efficient.[20] The kinship system may be transferred from the extended family to the nuclear family, often because such a system of smaller units fits more closely into the technical aspects of the agricultural system. For example, a system of land ownership and farming may employ a superfluity of people to produce a given crop. This gives

[20] Ralph Linton, "Cultural and Personality Factors Affecting Economic Growth," *Progress of Underdeveloped Areas,* ed. by B. F. Hoslitz (Chicago: University of Chicago Press, 1952), p. 82.

jobs to the extended family members. It also gives jobs to carpenters to keep the plows in order. An iron plow might destroy this cultural complex by denying jobs to carpenters and requiring less people on the farm.

The profitability of the technological improvement is not merely the amount of additional goods produced as a result of the introduction of the iron plow. Success is measured in the ability of the other institutions which are dependent upon the technical one, or related to it, to adjust themselves so that unemployment does not become endemic in the community.[21] This consideration requires that "the raising of living standards must always be a long-time project, with advances proceeding stage by stage."[22] The rule that Hogbin suggests is "innovations that a community accepts voluntarily are only potentially disruptive. The people will act as agents and may in consequence be able to achieve social integration."[23]

The points of interest are now clear for our discussion of cultural diffusion as the essence of the administration of technical assistance. The anthropologists teach us that change requires certain conditions for its success. The requirements listed below are not all-inclusive, but each situation carries its own peculiarities. Nevertheless, these generalizations are instructive.

> 1) Change must be in accord with, or at least not repulsive to, the indigenous value systems. Legitimation and the charter of institutions cannot be upset to a great degree unless chaos and disintegration are the desired immediate results. If orderly change is desired, the new factors must be acceptable, not only in terms of their technology, but also of their value. Social tensions in themselves do not necessarily inhibit change but may hasten it.

> 2) Institutional arrangements must not be drastically upset by an innovation. A drastic change is one that frustrates basic institutional behavior. The interrelations of institutions must be considered so that the fabric of society is not torn so that it fails to function.

> 3) Respected and authoritative personalities often are re-

---

21 Hogbin, *op. cit.*, p. 68.
22 *Ibid.*, p. 76.
23 *Ibid.*, p. 98.

quired to sanction and lead the introduction of technological change. This amounts to a person putting the seal of legitimacy on the change. His own personality, his arguments, or his example may be the living symbol of the acceptability of the change.

4) One change almost invariably implies others. The process of change, therefore, must be staged in some orderly fashion so that the process of change itself becomes accepted.

5) All these pieces of anthropological advice involve knowledge and empathy on the part of the administrators. Without such knowledge of and empathy for the social setting, and the setting of people and institutions, which are at the same time the subjects and objects of social change, frustration and chaos are likely to result.

The discussion of the experiences of technical assistance officials and technical assistance experiences in the following chapters is an attempt to examine the conditions and nature of change from the viewpoint of the actors and events.

II. Technical Aid—Who Really Does the Job?

(A Survey of the Opinions of U.S. Technicians)

Assistance to the developing countries is an integral part of the foreign policy of the United States. It is almost inconceivable that any federal administration in the next generation will fail to implement some sort of aid program for underdeveloped countries whose economic and political potentials are significant. The emphasis of U.S. aid may shift, and indeed is always in flux, but the fact of U.S. intervention to assist certain poorer countries in their technological development is settled policy. The amount of the budget devoted to technical assistance and the moral and political justifications will undoubtedly undergo change and adjustment to meet changing circumstances and pressures.

Such changes already are occurring and have been evolving since the inception of the program advanced in President Truman's famous 1949 Point IV statement in his inaugural address. The political atmosphere within the United States, reactions to American foreign policy by other nations, including the emerging nations, and American reactions to Soviet, Chinese, and Western European policies have had a bearing in changing the orientation of U.S. foreign aid. Of equal significance has been the political and social development in the underdeveloped countries themselves.

One aspect of the evolving policy which is attracting attention is the appropriate balance between economic aid in the form of development funds to finance capital and commodity imports on the one hand, and technical assistance in the form of training, advice, and demonstration on the other. Although the two forms of aid are inseparable, they may be used in varying proportions. The former is, of course, the more expensive and receives a larger share of U.S. aid spending.

20

Grants, largely Food for Peace (Public Law 480) and development loans, have in recent years exceeded $2 billion a year. The large Food for Peace allocations, more than $1.6 billion a year, obviously augment the food supplies of recipients (though P.L.480 has sometimes been viewed as a domestic farm aid mechanism). Regardless of the internal U.S. justification, the result is an economic transfer to the poor nations. Development loans have approached $900 million in recent years. Technical cooperation, which is mainly assistance, has cost approximately $200 million. Peace Corps expenditures (a type of technical assistance) are estimated at $105 million for 1966. These figures, however, do not fully indicate the financial participation of the United States. The Alliance for Progress, various United Nations bodies, the Monetary Fund, and the International Bank are among other commitments; yet technical-assistance expenditures are rather small compared to total U.S. expenditures for international cooperative organizations and foreign economic assistance.

Foreign assistance is but one cord which binds the United States to the rest of the world. Technical assistance, from the viewpoint of United States policy, is an important strand in that cord and is becoming more important as time goes on.

The full implications of the foreign assistance program and its likely changes are not yet clearly visible. No one, however, will be able to sense even the major implications of the policy unless he has some conception of popular motivations, the likely effects of given programs, the probable role of personality in social change, and other significant factors which influence society. Indeed, unless we estimate the dimensions of the future—or better still, the possible alternative futures of the world—we are unable to evaluate, even approximately, the final results of foreign assistance.

But no one can know the future with any exactitude. At best, we can guess and estimate. We thus operate, of necessity, in ignorance and with estimates. It is ignorance which so often gives us the happy illusion of the freedom of choice of the alternative policies and programs by which we hope to affect the course of events.

These remarks sound like a vague, philosophical, and academic commentary on the difficulties and uncertainties of foreign policy. But, vague or not, knowledge in the sphere of the effects of foreign aid is not exact. In brief, we do not know the future, nor do we know how to control and fashion it. Efforts are only partly based on sound knowledge of cause and effect. Guess and ignorance are ingredients in the policy.

THE MANY FACES OF TECHNICAL ASSISTANCE

To be effective, political action must be both tentative and flexible. But the necessity of making commitments sometimes makes flexible action impossible. The means of achieving goals must be in accord with the times and personalities involved. Ends sought must be ranked in terms of their importance and their position in the sequence of events which are peculiar to the society in question.

Tools to achieve the ends of a policy must work within given limitations. The tools are the means, the programs; but programs are on paper and need to be implemented by people with knowledge and technique. It is at the level of the program that most of the current technical interest has been centered. The technician is the individual charged with bringing about the cultural diffusion decided by higher administration. He accepts the policy which guides him, but he operates in an institutional complex which is only partially known to him and rarely fully understood. He must work in his own mission with people constrained by other technical training and with their own restraints. He must also work with technicians of the recipient country who are bound by an entirely different set of institutional and value restraints and who may view the program quite differently from the way the American technician views it. The American technician, for his part, views the program as his policy goal.

The counterpart technician may, for his part, view the program as a means in an entirely different policy orientation. For example, the American who is concerned about health improvement may measure his success objectively by the number of antibiotic injections or the decline in the mortality rate. But his counterpart may see the program not as an end in itself, but as a means for improving the labor force to secure men for the army, or as a means for securing a greater output of food *via* better health, or possibly even as a step toward a better job in the Ministry of Health. The American technician may understand these other considerations, but to him they are extraneous.

A U.S. agricultural expert and his counterpart may have as an instructional guideline the increase in production of a given crop. Their effort to help the peasant farmers may be successful, yet the implications of an increased yield may be the beginning of a whole new series of problems to the host country technician. If the peasants cannot sell the additional product because of the smallness of the market, lack of roads, or insufficiency of transportation, frustration may be the price of success. Even if the increased crop yield is profitably sold, the final outcome may depend on whether or not the farmers find something to buy with their increased income. The additional income may be spent on a wedding or invested in equipment. A successful experiment may open Pandora's box, but the U.S. technician does not need to face the problems which fly out. It is his counterpart, rather, or his counterpart's agency, which will have to overcome the newly created problems.

Indeed, the desire of the farmers for increased income may be viewed as an increased demand for specific types of services which might vary from leisure on the one hand to lottery tickets on the other, with all degrees of saving, investment and consumption in between. Program or policy from the U.S. viewpoint tends to be narrower than from the viewpoint of the host administration.

To the U.S. technician, the policy is already set. As the program upon which he is working proceeds, the technician hopes that the total result will be favorable. Without such hope the technician is frustrated, for he is not responsible for the whole world but only his part of it. In truth, however, his segment has meaning only in terms of the totality. The uncertainty about the meshing of the entire program and doubts about the meaningfulness of the immediate program in totality often disturb government technicians.

THE IMAGE OF THE TECHNICIANS

Granting that the technician can be concerned only with his part of the larger process, the commitment and attitude of the technician remain as important considerations. To whom does he owe his loyalty and devotion? How does he view himself, how is he viewed by his superiors and by the power elite of the host country? Is he viewed as a professional dedicated only to the job and without any particular political orientation? Is he viewed merely as a person "in business for himself," doing a job and getting by, possibly having taken the foreign assignment to enjoy the excitement and perquisites of a foreign post?

Obviously, different personalities view themselves and are viewed differently in varying situations and under different conditions of public and private tension. It is also likely that different tasks imply different degrees of dedication to job, home country, self, and recipient country. The technician engaged in advising ways and means to take a census or prepare a budget need not have the same motivation and dedication as a person engaged in fighting an epidemic. The type of person who is an advisor on manpower or industrial relations might be successful, although his dedication and commitment are unlike that of an advisor on tax reform or road building.

These hypothetical examples are at the level of program. At the level of program integration, policy considerations both at the technical and political levels are even more complex and subtle.

AN AID STUDY

The Agency for International Development (AID) attempted to secure insights on the kind of problems we have been considering through an internal study. A study group, established in the fall of 1959, was instructed to isolate and evaluate the factors which should govern the nature, size, techniques, and administration of future technical assistance programs, until more long-term research should provide more scientifically grounded guidelines. The small task force was handicapped by the loss of interest in the program by the administration in power. At its peak the staff consisted of only seven professional employees, but these people had had much experience overseas in AID and its predecessor agencies. Their long report consists largely of excerpts from interviews with about 1,100 individuals. These individuals were International Cooperation Administration (ICA) technicians returning home from leave for consultation or reassignment (350); other ICA employees returning home from leave for consultation or reassignment (200); employees of participating agencies (200); Washington employees of ICA and AID who had previously served overseas (220); individuals who had experience overseas in foundations, universities, business concerns, etc., but who were not associated with the U.S.

government (100); and employees of international organizations, other governments or foreign private organizations (50). Official cables, reports, and in some instances magazine or press articles were included as references.

The interviews were extensive, running for two hours or more, and were not structured, allowing the person being interviewed to speak freely on any aspect of technical assistance to which he thought he could contribute. Each interview was analyzed by subject into a complex classification system. A single excerpt (subject) which had several aspects was classified under each subject or question to which it was thought to apply. For example, an answer which held that the "first qualification of a technician is his ability to get along with people" was filed under the heading of his ability (1) to project himself into another situation, (2) to understand and like people, and (3) to get along with people. The same observation was also considered important to the consideration of whether technical competence is less important than certain other qualities. The unbounded zeal of the staff to view every facet of technical aid led them to create an analytic device which is monumental, but the monument is, in many cases, too great for the substance of the interviews.

No evaluation of the responses is offered in the study although the reader can make something of an evaluation because the rank and experience in overseas areas of each respondent are given for each excerpted paragraph. The reader, however, has no way of judging the objectivity on the validity of each response. What the reader can ascertain is the frequency with which certain ideas are expressed. One must be on his guard, of course, against assuming that a point of view expressed with frequency is necessarily a correct one from the standpoint of the efficient administration of technical assistance.

The persons interviewed were, by and large, American technicians in the employ of the federal government or American foundations and business firms. They present what amounts to an American point of view. The reaction of the host technicians and politicians to the attitudes, work, and personality of the American technicians is not considered. We have, therefore, what amounts to a half survey: a survey of the Americans giving their ideas of what a good technician or an effective technical aid program is or should be. We do not know from the data what the counterpart technicians think about the same subject. It is as if a market survey were based entirely on the reactions of salesmen to a market situation, and not on the reactions of the buyers. Good, sensitive salesmen do know something about the nature of the market and the attitude of buyers, but the buyers' reactions are not directly known.

WHAT THE DATA SHOW—AN UNOBTAINABLE IDEAL

The remainder of this chapter is concerned with drawing some inferences and conclusions from the contents of two volumes of the AID study. These volumes are concerned with personal qualities needed by technicians and the general approach to technical assistance.

The volumes were chosen for this discussion because they deal with psychological or socio-psychological considerations. The personal-qualities aspect deals essentially with what the technicians believe are good and bad characteristics of their craft and profession. The general-approach aspect deals with the psychological relations between technicians and their counterparts or the indigenous people, which in turn lead to the success or frustration of technical assistance programs.

Since these studies are not available to the public, footnotes and other signals of reference will not be made. Countries will be designated only by reference to general areas, e.g., continents or regions.

According to the study the personal qualities required in technicians working on technical assistance are by no means limited to technical competence. The list of qualities in addition to technical ones includes such nontechnical considerations as dedication or missionary zeal, spiritual qualities, capacity to motivate people, capacity for leadership, capacity to communicate with other people, ability to teach or train, ability to project oneself into another situation, to understand and like people, to get along with people, capacity to instill confidence in other people, integrity, capacity to organize and manage, sophistication and broad understanding, flexibility, resourcefulness, patience, nature, tact and diplomacy, tolerance, and lack of prejudice.

As one would expect, the overwhelming tenor of the comments is that technicians, in addition to having technical competence, should be decent people, considerate of others, willing to listen patiently, but not utterly without backbone. They should be sophisticated and understanding but should always exercise tact. Indeed, one might infer that the ideal person is also the ideal technician. Some of the ideal qualifications are in conflict. For example, one program officer with experience in Africa suggests that persons of missionary zeal are not appropriate, yet another educational officer with experience in the same area suggests that great dedication and an extreme interest in people make for effectiveness in the field. Still another official suggests that a dedicated technician with only mediocre ability can be more effective than his highly qualified colleague who lacks dedication.

Apparently, the technician must thus be a man with great but not excessive zeal, and with high competence unless his lack of competence is offset by his dedication. In addition to his own inspiration and sense of mission, he must be able to inspire confidence in others, according to a technician with experience in Southeast Asia. He should be able to "identify himself with the local communities" and possess humility, according to the report of an African hand. It is clear from these characteristics, which obviously were not chosen at random but to show the complexity of personality requirements, that it is highly unlikely that any one person employed as a technician can at all times and under all circumstances satisfy the ideal which all the responding officials consider necessary. One cannot object to the comments of the respondents to the interviews. Each comment has an air of truth and ring of sincerity about it and is undoubtedly based upon the personal experience and observation of the respondent.

The quotation from former Assistant Secretary of State Harlan Cleveland's article, "Representation of the U.S. Abroad," sums up the ideal technician from the viewpoint of technicians in the field. Cleveland writes:

> A person ought to have the requisite skill for the job he does; [he] needs versatility and willingness to improvise, knowledge of his field and an attitude toward it, a belief in mission and dedication to his work that enables him to survive repeated frustrations and yet retain his zest for the job; the sensitivity to see himself as a political man, whose actions or inactions affect the power structure around him; cultural empathy, the

curiosity to study and the skill to perceive the inner logic and coherence of another's way of thinking, plus the restraint not to judge it as bad because it is different from our way; organization ability which is partly tolerance for large-scale bureaucracy and an understanding of the complex administrative relationships between headquarters and the field talent for building institutions, which means essentially the talent for teaching other people to take your place.

Such people are hard to find, especially since, according to a technician who has worked in North Africa, the official ought to have a wife who is willing and able to serve overseas!

Undesirable characteristics are also cited. Here again the characteristics which are purported to lead technicians to failure in overseas assignments may be viewed as stereotypes which lead people to failure in almost any environment. Undesirable characteristics include impoliteness, authoritarian personality traits, "skirt chasing," drinking, an impersonal tourist attitude rather than one of dedication and commitment, impatience, a desire to get away from family, an inability to communicate, and the adoption of a superior "colonial administrator complex."

Probably of greater interest in understanding the qualities which technicians believe they need bring to the task is contained in the sections of the report devoted to regions and countries.

Specific Attributes

It appears that where the technical capacity of the indigenous technician is low, the U.S. technician need not be of the highest rank; but on the other hand, his capacity to persuade the local people, and to improvise, should be of a high order. In South-Asia, technical competence and prestige seem to be the necessary characteristics for foreign technicians. These countries have had a long experience with British civil servants and British education. Where the host technician is highly competent, the U.S. technician, if he is to be successful, needs to be very competent with reputable scientific, technical, and academic status. In countries which are sensitive to the color problem, the qualifications of the technician, if he is to be successful, must include the capacity to get along with indigenous people, and above all a feeling of mutuality for the colored people. The strong nationalism of Africans requires an interest in Africa on the part of the U.S. technician, as well as an interest in technology.

In road building, for example, it is suggested that the U.S. experience of fifty years ago is valuable, since the conditions in many developing countries are similar to those of the United States in the past. It is also apparent, however, that modern road-building equipment and modern engineering may be used anywhere. U.S. know-how of the present is useful in the emerging societies.

Public Health technicians with experience in Central America report that technical advisors should be inventive. Reliance upon the prevailing techniques of the United States is not always possible because the local resources are simply insufficient to permit the imitation of up-to-date American procedures.

Insofar as education is concerned, a study of the characteristics of the most and least effective educational advisors serving overseas indicates that successful educational technicians have had practical experience in addition to possessing positive personality characteristics. Educational administrators or persons trained in educational administration had more success than educational technicians. Men in the age group of 36 to 55, particularly in the younger range, tended to show more flexibility and adaptability than older men.

In the area of housing, according to an official with experience in South America, advisors should have imagination, initiative, and above all a capacity to see the housing problem as a social, political, regional, and financial problem, and not merely as a technical one. U.S. public housing experience is not always applicable overseas, according to a housing specialist with experience in Central America, Eastern Europe, and Southeast Asia.

An interesting remark is made with respect to economic advisors by one who has served in Europe and Asia. His reaction is that young technically trained economists, rather than older men with reputations, are desirable. This is because the younger economists in the recipient country tend to be skilled in modern analytic techniques and respect a similar up-to-date skill in their counterparts. This reaction differs from the more general one that prestige often makes the technician acceptable in the more scientifically advanced host countries.

The excerpts also assert that the families of technicians play an important role in their acceptance and effectiveness. Wives and children are significant not only in the contacts they make but also in the problems they bring. Large families require special schooling arrangements and living provisions which are often difficult to secure. A family which integrates itself into the local society may help the technical aid program, while the family which holds itself aloof or has friction with the local population may create serious problems.

Praise and Blame

A type of institutional problem which is of concern to the reporting American technician is that of "kudos" or who gets the credit for successes. Clearly, in a responsible and responsive government, the administration must take the blame for failure, as well as the praise for success of its efforts. Where technical assistance is being given by the United States, two sovereign nations are acting together and therefore sharing responsibility. The praise which the United States or its officials might receive for a job well done or the blame for a job poorly done is not only recorded in the United States, it is also recorded in the country in which the action takes place. U.S. officials abroad are exposed and in competition with host country officials for either praise or blame. How to share credit or blame in the host country so that the technical program is benefited is a question which involves the political psychology of both countries.

Does it help U.S. policy and future international relations if the host country takes all or part of the praise or, conversely, of the blame? Under most circumstances the technicians believe that the U.S. should not seek credit but strengthen the hand of the host government and its technicians by allowing them to take credit for a job well done. The reasoning is that this enhances the view that the foreign country is independent of the U.S. "domination." On the other hand, there is the feeling that the man on the street—the ordinary person—should know the extent to which he and his nation are being helped by the United States. In some instances it is pointed out that it is undesirable to have ordinary citizens realize how close their government works with the United States. The case in point is a regime which is decidedly unpopular. Playing down praise may play down blame of failure.

A single policy, of course, is not applicable to all cases, but most of the respondents believe that the role of the United States should be to serve quietly, and that virtue is its own reward. Nevertheless, the educated and power elites of the society should be made aware of the contribution of the United States. A series of program successes, if known, makes it more likely that the host government will cooperate fully in future undertakings.

Some commentators point out that the very nature of some programs causes the United States to become popular with the so-called man in the street. This is true of purely altruistic programs such as earthquake relief, public housing, or the extermination of malaria. Usually such activity is made known not through any propaganda devices, but by the value and success of the programs themselves.

Effectiveness of the assistance effort may not be due to the particular powers or capacities of the technician but to the particular division of labor employed. The failure of American technicians and host technicians to separate system or organizational efficiency from personal efficiency may lead to a loss of pride and face. Indeed, one U.S. observer who had experience in Asia remarked that among the obstacles to development are "inferiority complexes" in the recipient population. To the American technician, novel social organizations and training may indicate that foreigners suffer from an inferior social system rather than that the system is being adjusted to do a task for which it was not devised.

Nearly all technicians agree that one must be sensitive and have empathy for the pride and value systems of the recipient countries. This is easier said than done. Recognition of the obvious technical superiority of the West to the non-West is often traumatic for the educated elite of the recipient countries, for in asking for help they reveal their own inadequacy. The feeling of superiority of the U.S. technician may express itself as a teacher-student relationship between the technician and his opposite number, as a patronizing attitude in the role of advisor, or by a lecturing attitude. No single prescription is available to avoid such improper attitudes. Patience, by itself a virtue so often suggested by some respondents, is not enough for others, because patience allowed to run indefinitely becomes tired and accepts inferior performance. Allowing the host country personnel to entertain exaggerated expectations is as harmful as letting improprieties slide by.

Experts who have worked in the programs of Latin America, Asia, South Europe, and North Africa indicate that short-term demonstration programs may have a good effect only in the villages or local areas where the demonstrations take place. For the long pull and for a broad effect more general institutional approaches are more likely to work. The demonstration technique is only part of the institutional changing and building techniques in the minds of many respondents. That a feeling of technical inferiority with respect to modern equipment may create a sense of awe in the illiterate farmer need be only a short-run phenomenon. The success of mechanized equipment all over the world indicates that the technology is not very difficult to learn.

Politics and Purpose

The ideological and political setting of technical assistance is of significance. The immediate operational questions come down to such considerations as: How should the U.S. technician act, given the setting and situation in which he finds himself? What do the recipient nation's technicians think of U.S. policy and the individuals with whom they come in contact? What sort of social behavior is acceptable and what is not? How can the U.S. image be improved? Is there a difference between the American motives and the recipient nation's conception of them?

Underlying these questions is the fact of Communism. Deep in the consciousness of American technicians, and probably of all people in the world, is the belief that U.S. policy is one of the restraints against Communism. U.S. policy is often believed to be based on U.S. concern with the dual threat of the Soviet Union and Red China. This view is endemic in spite of the ideological rationalization that American aid programs are determined by mutuality of purpose and that U.S. interests are in accord with the interests of the recipient nations. The idea of international mutuality of interest is not easy to explain to people who consider themselves recipients rather than partners. After all, what difference does it make to the United States, or to the world at large, if a remote village has a well with clean water, or if some chain of villages develop farm-to-market roads. Yet these are the sorts of programs which require legitimation by mutuality of interest.

An official with experience in Asia points out that it is important to convince the people of recipient nations that their own welfare and the welfare of the United States are mutually interdependent, and that U.S. and host purposes coincide! Other officials point out that U.S. purposes are not clear to the recipients, and a review of them is therefore necessary. The view that U.S. purposes must be clarified to U.S. personnel and host personnel is frequently held. Merely to exhort the peoples of the developing world to have faith in American altruism is not likely to be successful. Some person, such as the Catholic priest in Nepal who is dedicated to the local population, can make his point by his personal behavior. But this takes a lifetime of special behavior and a well-appointed institution, with permanence. U.S. government agencies, or U.S. personnel, are not likely to meet such requirements.

All programs, however, do not require such complex political and moral justifications. An official who has worked in Southeast Asia as a sanitary engineer and public health expert points out "in public health generally and in malaria eradication particularly, it is essential that people understand what it is that the program is trying to accomplish." He, therefore, places a high value on publicity and education. The eradication of malaria, however, is different from political and social reform. It would seem that programs categorized as nonpolitical in the minds of recipient peoples have a better chance of acceptance than programs which may involve more subtle "political" overtones.

Technical assistance often presents a dilemma, as a Harvard University respondent points out, because the United States may simultaneously be seeking conflicting objectives, viz., promotion of local government stability along with economic changes. But the continuance of the limited, narrow power structure may cause the liberals of the host country to become disillusioned and to think that the United States is not really interested in progress. Another question which concerns the respondent technicians is: With whom should the United States be working? Should it work with the group in power, or should it work with, and so support, other elites who are seeking power? An official who served in South and Southeast Asia points out that one cannot avoid working with groups already in power, but limiting one's attention to them places all one's eggs in a single political basket. One must develop some identification with the "out" groups, while continuing to seek a base in popular support.

The discussion of the technicians moves from a relatively high political level to a more operational level. As three experts from the U.S. Department of Health, Education and Welfare point out, great advantages would accrue to the United States from promoting close professional ties between U.S. technicians and host technicians in the host government ministries and elsewhere. Individual associations between people of similar technical interests already exist and should be built upon. A network of friendship would be of enormous value, i.e., a network of friendship between similarly dedicated professional technicians.

Is Assistance Contractual?

Assuming that the hurdles of priorities, sovereignty priorities, and political implications are jumped, how does one secure detailed understandings and agreements between the United States and the host governments? Here the choice of being hard-boiled or permissive must be faced. One can reduce all agreements to writing so that the specific obligations and rights are laid out, or alternatively one can "play it by ear."

It is argued by many of the respondents that clear-cut, initial understandings with respect to the way a program is to be carried out, and the mutual responsibilities and obligations of the contracting parties, are essential. Some go so far as to argue that all agreements should be reduced to writing, because people in foreign lands, especially those of the underdeveloped countries, have respect for written contracts. Furthermore, the foreign officials expect to bargain because that is their way of life.

More moderate commentators suggest that basic guide lines for technical assistance with standards and techniques of review be instituted. An official who has worked in Africa and Asia suggests that detailed project agreements are desirable insofar as they afford protection to the host technicians against higher ministerial officials involved in the project. This, however, is quite different from putting the entire understanding and procedure in the form of a contract to be interpreted legalistically.

A possible idea in the back of the mind of the many respondents who suggest written agreements is the desire to have a handy means of legitimating technical assistance actions for themselves and their colleagues. The written contract, it is believed, because of its official appearance, provides them with a charter for action which is not inherent in less formal understandings. Some of the respondents suggest that in addition to a written contract there should be a clear understanding concerning certain basic facts or conditions which are necessary for the successful operation of a program, e.g., the training of local personnel and phasing out of U.S. personnel, and the provision of certain resources of capital and personnel by the recipient country. This proposition is quite distinct from the rigid and demanding contractual arrangement. Indeed, some of the commentators argue that the contractual arrangement destroys the ideal that the program is one for the recipient country, and that the United States is only providing help. Others point out that "getting tough" with the host ministries or agencies does not assure that the personnel involved will capitulate to American toughness.

But deeper than the issue of being hardboiled or permissive is the question of why there is an inability or refusal on the part of the foreign country to meet the commitments which they make. Leaving out the political aspect, which may be significant and upon which the technicians did not comment, a point is made by several technicians that the administrative machinery and competence of an underdeveloped country are often so meager that the country cannot carry out its obligations. Such countries are trying to do too much, and they simply are not able to do what they desire or plan to do. This is reported for the Middle East and Asia and is implied in South America. It is also suggested that programs may conflict with each other since the requirements of *all* the programs are in excess of a nation's available resources.

To improve the intellectual and social climate is at best a long-run goal, but a necessary one in the opinion of many of the commentators. The experts suggest, with insight, that at least some of the technical aid programs are accepted by the underdeveloped countries because they are a necessary step for these countries to secure other kinds of U.S. aid in material goods which, they fear, will not be forthcoming without the technical assistance program.

1410876

III. Experiences in Agriculture

(The AID Study Continued)

The experience of the technicians in agriculture was summarized in a separate report. The summary is organized with the idea of placing information about agricultural technical assistance in one package. In this report the role of technical cooperation in agriculture is defined as "all of these activities (other than the importation of capital) which aim primarily at developing a more productive agriculture in a country and in which an outside . . . agency is a cooperating partner."

According to many respondents, one of the more basic dysfunctions of underdeveloped society appears to be the reluctance of *local* technicians to assume responsibility for the adoption of new practices. A concurrent feature of this fear is the culturally determined or perhaps "elitist" distaste for working with one's hands. Such reluctance of host technicians and administrations to participate wholeheartedly is often marked by the lack of desire to pass on existing technical information to farmers. This is so either because the applicability of the information is believed to be suspect, or the host administrators and technicians do not sufficiently understand its content to be able to explain it to the farmers and, therefore, fear a "loss of face." The result is a continuation of former behavior patterns. U.S. advisors point out such difficulties in agricultural technical assistance programs in diverse nations in Asia, Africa, South America, and Eastern Europe. A reluctance to attempt new practices is similar the world over, presumably because of the risks involved in the adoption of novel techniques and values. Such attitudes are often present when a one-crop subsistence-type agriculture is the dominant feature of the economic and social system in which innovation is desired.

The persistence of a method of performance regardless of technical or other changes is not confined to the administrators and technicians of nations receiving U.S. technical assistance in agriculture. Many of the personnel sent abroad as "innovators" are themselves not predisposed to innovation, and probably do not understand the subtleties of innovation—especially when it comes to the adaptation of institutions into a new economic and social milieu. An example is an agricultural program in Africa, which failed to train local personnel, and was still American-run after many years of operation. Another example is that of a U.S. Operations Mission to a Southeast Asian nation. The USOM believed that the farmers were not yet "ready" for an irrigation cooperative, with the result that the United States persisted in maintaining the irrigation project after the timetable required U.S. withdrawal.

An underlying philosophy of many programs seems to be that U.S. institutions are transferable to underdeveloped lands. There is, nevertheless, a conscious realization that replicas of U.S. institutions cannot be imposed on countries without adaptations which the facts of the situation require. For example, in a South Asian country the introduction of the land-grant college was not an effective approach to the over-all problem of agricultural extension. The attempt appears to have been designed to infuse the American concept of extension work into a local extension system which was different in fundamental aspects from its U.S. counterpart. A more realistic approach might have been to examine more carefully the provincial agriculture programs to which the nation's extension was tied, rather than to attempt to supply personnel trained in the functioning of an alien U.S. system. In this respect it was proposed by one observer that U.S. agricultural colleges and the Department of Agriculture develop ways to transmit knowledge of improved agriculture to farmers in less-developed countries, *within the framework of the cultural and economic conditions which exist in the countries.* Such programs require a working understanding of the host country's system of values, economic status, and organization, as well as its patterns of thinking and administrative procedures. Policies and practices indigenous to United States often failed or were weak in the dissemination of information and assistance concerning such commodities as cotton, rice, and grains in the countries of Latin America, Africa, and South Asia.

The use of P.L.480 surplus grain for livestock feed between 1954 and 1958 in an African society resulted in a 7 per cent increase in range livestock. The result was that the livestock population grew beyond that which the range could sustain, even with bountiful rainfall. The program of range feeding drastically upset the balance of nature and the increases in the herds. This error was inherent in the utilization of U.S. surplus grain. It might have been more in the host's interest to have allocated the gift grain to a program of fattening livestock just prior to slaughter. The latter plan is a U.S. institution which might have been realistically transferred to and adopted in the local institutional complex with a minimum of resistance and a maximum of benefit. The uncritical use of an existing practice destroyed the effectiveness of what was essentially a pragmatic innovation.

Another manifestation of pattern-maintenance, or rigidity, has been encountered by U.S. personnel in South Asia, West Africa, and the Caribbean, where colonial traditions and influences are strong because of expatriate personnel in administrative positions. When U.S. technical assistance in extension was frustrated by European expatriates in administrative positions in an African state, the Mission undertook performance-type technical assistance to demonstrate U.S. skills to the government and to the farmers. Only then was it possible to advise at the national level. Another example was the prevailing strong British tradition in the Caribbean, which rejected agricultural extension. The local college of agriculture was directly tied to London University and presumably was designed to serve plantation interests. The U.S. advisors suggested that the college should have been persuaded to perform a new service function to isolated farmers.

In South and Central America, another form of pattern-maintenance was evident in U.S. and local agricultural technical assistance programs. In one instance the United States was accused of dominating a program because of its insistence that its financial contribution should permit certain administrative privileges. This led to conflicts with local nationalists. In another experience, U.S. participation was identified by the masses with programs that made the rich richer, because the subsistence farmers were not greatly affected by the technical assistance programs. Another technician with experience in Latin America commented that U.S. officials should be more careful in the future about attaching a radical label to persons who merely want to improve the lot of the Indians by agrarian reform. Such individuals were branded as Communists, a fact which precluded the effectiveness of the U.S. program. Private and religious agencies also engaged in agrarian reform were similarly restrained.

The agricultural summary report notes that Latin American representatives are seriously concerned with land reform in terms of such practical considerations as credit, access roads, research, and extension. It was noted that it is not the responsibility of the United States to carry out these programs, but the United States must provide the assistance so that the developing societies can carry out the programs themselves. It should be remembered, however, that institutional change and technical innovation require people; technicians and leaders break the settled ground of change and secure acceptance for themselves and their programs.

A few examples are indicative of alternative techniques to help agriculture. In a Middle Eastern village project, the government took an inventory of the village resources which were available for experimentation. It financed with AID support one pilot project, which included advice and capital resources, in each of a number of villages. In other villages, the government and AID supplied only improved seed and other factors which were not locally available. Both projects were reported to be extremely successful, suggesting the need and usefulness of new resources as well as the psychological implications of advice.

The reduction of land rents in a Far Eastern country frequently meant a wide enough financial margin for the tenant to enable him to build his own house, buy livestock, marry, and plan for the future. Moreover, it gave the tenant more incentive to improve the land. In North Africa, the trucks of a land resettlement project were used to transport vegetables to city markets as an incentive for farmers to raise vegetables, which demonstrated their profitability when commercial transportation was available.

Since most farm units in the less-developed countries are family owned and operated and not commercial, in the American sense, the production of crops is often not carried out on a basis of market profitability, but on their usefulness for family consumption. An awareness of the farmers that they need not be bound by traditional practices, but can make new decisions, is contagious. The objective of the "pilot area" approach in a Southeast Asian state was to increase the purchasing power of farmers through concentration on one or two cash crops resulting from the upgrading of subsistence production. This same objective was stressed in a West African society.

In a Pacific country, the farmers were known to be more concerned with what their neighbors tried to do than in what experimental stations claimed to have done, or in what extension workers claimed to be able to do for them. The best approach, therefore, was to assist a few local farmers in carrying on demonstrations on their own farms while other farmers watched, and later copied, the novel techniques. Yet one can exaggerate the role of demonstration. In some cases there are limits to the demonstration effect because of a psychological unwillingness to accept change. Sometimes the effect is limited to a small area and does not spread. No single approach is universal.

Research can make a genuine contribution when coupled with realistic extension programs. One successful Far Eastern research project based the experimental rates of fertilizer and lime application upon (1) what the crops required for the best growth and, more importantly, (2) on the ability of farmers to purchase fertilizer and lime.

In the examples cited above, novelty of purpose was supported by institutional change, i.e., innovation of means. The new goals set for the farmer permitted a change in his behavior. The new setting reduced the latency of the old setting.

It was generally recommended by technician respondents that when a culture has not developed adaptive flexibility, technical assistance should concentrate on improving the existing implements and agricultural practices. Effort should not be directed to introducing new types of implements and practices during the early stages of innovation. In an East African state where fishing was previously performed by hand lines from dugout canoes, a project purpose was to introduce, demonstrate, and train the fishermen in the use of modern methods and techniques with long-line fishing gear, set lines, gill nets, lobster traps, and motorized fishing boats. It is significant to note that the people in a fishing village once stoned a motorized fishing boat because they thought it was catching fish they otherwise would have caught. By the following season, however, the fishermen had accepted the new technique and became enthusiastic to the point of trying to obtain more boats. In a South American land, the attempted introduction of electronic sonar gear to "sound" for schools of fish resulted in equipment lying idle in government storerooms. Yet cases can be cited in which modern equipment was so useful that it was quickly taken up by farmers, e.g., irrigation equipment in a Middle Eastern state.

In developing societies, the needs for agricultural development are often met not so much by the demonstration of technical alternatives as by the fostering of new ways of thinking and acting. Where a government earnestly desires to improve agricultural production and gives it necessary priority, obstacles to improved production have been overcome. For example, a West African irrigation project was very popular with the masses. It directly benefited them by opening roads by which they could get goods more cheaply while reducing the walking distance to water in the dry season. The maintenance of their livestock and certain crops was also assured. An agricultural credit policy in a Middle Eastern Society reduced landlord orientation through government action. The new policy also fostered local confidence in the government through government action. The new policy also fostered local confidence in the government through the realization that someone in authority desired to help the local cultivator.

A university commentator believes that "our tendency is to emphasize projects rather than *general* programs which tackle, through related and coordinated projects, the complex of problems confronting a country in a particular field. Programs have fallen flat in agriculture in many countries for this reason." An example of the failure to consider the full implications of coordinated projects was shown in one North African country by the inability to win the confidence of the appropriate government officials. Since the focus of U.S. assistance was upon training extension workers and not in adapting the system to the more general social and political requirement, it received little government assistance. The program emphasis was demonstrated in a South American country when the change of price controls (one project) led to increased interest and activity in livestock improvement (another project). The successful program was the interaction of two projects.

Successful cultural and technical diffusion in the experience of the reporting technicians does not mean that they transplanted a way of acting and organization successfully used in the United States to a foreign environment. It means that they adapted the organization of the United States to the local setting and local values or that they improvised a new set of organizational ideas and tools. The point is that novel means (organization and behavior) and ends have to be functional in the environment, even if this implies adjusting the environment. Communication and management then are crucial. Insofar as technical aid tries to emphasize advice, the importance of organization goals and local resources are of utmost importance in environmental and goal adjustment.

The examples and comments of agricultural technicians concerned with technical aid seem to point out that:

(1) Technical aid does not, *de novo,* introduce rationality into agriculture, rather it improves knowledge, capital, and organization so as to produce a *new* rational pattern of action.

(2) Novel patterns of action often tend to be persistent when linked to new, effective projects elsewhere. Government, market, technical, advisory, and other institutions (the setting) must be linked to the new behavior patterns on the farm if the latter is to continue.

(3) Technical aid in the form of advice, demonstration, and vocational training is like any other capital investment. To be productive it must be goal-oriented. If the additional yields do not benefit the farmer through increased income or less effort, the technical aid will not become a part of the behavior pattern. Technical aid requires supportive changes in economic, government, and other institutions.

(4) Technical assistance personnel become, in effect, the temporary links between the agricultural institutions on the one side, and the setting of those institutions on the other.

In general the technical assistants suggest two bundles of conclusions. The first has to do with the orientation of the field people. As one would expect and hope, their first concern was with the job at hand. This narrow focus, however, was not satisfactory, since many, perhaps all, were concerned with the general process of development as well as with their own immediate tasks. Yet the interrelation of their responsibilities and operations with the larger strategy and operation seemed a worry rather than an inner security based on either faith or knowledge. Development as an ongoing strategy is not within the grasp of the respondents, so they were not always sure of their role in the total scheme. The second conclusion is more positive. The technicians suggested four crucial components of technical assistance:

(1) The level of education of the host population. This is an indication of the general level of economic and social development of the host. Different approaches are needed in countries of different educational levels.

(2) The level of administrative competence of the host. Again it is suggested that the cloth be cut to the pattern. Where public administration is of a high order, a different approach is needed than if the level of public administration is lower.

(3) The pool of technicians. If there are well-trained technicians in sufficient number, the kind and number of U.S. technicians is in a changing relative proportion to the kind and number in a land with a small pool of technicians.

(4) Personality characteristics of the U.S. technicians. In general the kind of U.S. technical people needed depends on the three other components.

IV. Some Cases of Technical Assistance Analyzed

Introduction

The success or failure of technical assistance programs and projects may be examined on at least two levels: (1) The immediate institutional and personnel level of operation; and (2) The setting (milieu) of the institution, including the linkages between the project being undertaken and the environment which surrounds it.

In the examination of the success or failure of a program, the setting and linkages should be examined only after an analysis of finance procedures and manpower fails to provide a persuasive explanation. Obvious reasons for conflicts and delays such as language barriers or lack of familiarity with the donor and host's administrative procedures are of great significance in determining the outcome of a program. These reasons may be considered procedural. Competition for manpower and funds between different projects in a developing society occurs frequently.

Technical assistance has been operationally defined by the International Institute of Administrative Sciences:

> Technical assistance consists in the transmission of learning, knowledge, and techniques or material and human resources in order to help those who receive it to solve specific problems in a more suitable manner in keeping with their needs. It is an external contribution which assumes a very wide variety of forms: visits of experts and technicians, receiving fellowship holders, organizing courses and seminars, exchanging or disseminating information or documents, and supplying material and equipment, and occasionally financial means.[1]

[1] *Technical Assistance in Public Administration: Lessons of Experience and Possible Improvements* (Vienna: International Institute of Administrative Sciences [XIIth International Congress], July, 1962), p. 12.

44

Technical assistance, if we accept this definition, thus consists of two parts: (1) transmission of knowledge through training and (2) transfer of material resources. The stress, however, is on knowledge and information, with material and financing being of secondary importance.

The primary data for this chapter consists of sixty-three reports prepared by AID field offices on technical assistance projects in Asia and Africa. The countries referred to in the text have, at the suggestion of AID, been designated by letters which have no necessary connection with the states' names. Where different cases refer to a given state, varying letters of identification have been used.

The quotations in this Chapter are from these Reports.

In Section II some typical situations of stress are discussed, and an attempt is made to identify the conditions under which these are likely to occur. Section III provides examples of procedural difficulties faced in the administrative process of technical aid.

To the administrator, procedural difficulties are considered part of the cultural environment, and he generally knows the ways to deal with them. A delay in decision-making by one's own legislature or administration is accepted as part of the game. A delay, however, by the legislature or supply office of a foreign nation may often be more difficult for the administrator to understand.

From these general considerations we move to the particular cases in Section IV (illustrative cases). In that section, cases have been grouped around a few important characteristics, and certain implications that follow are pointed out. The concluding section, Section V, examines some areas of agriculture and resource development. Section VI summarizes the Chapter.

SITUATIONS OF STRESS

The simplest cases of technical assistance to understand or evaluate are those in which the donor and host agree on the nature of the problem to be solved. This unity of purpose may be technical, e.g., it may be based on an aviation or hydroelectric project, or on a well-defined goal, e.g., trade union development. In such cases the process moves smoothly if the recipient country has capable and flexible persons in top positions of authority plus adequate personnel, administration, and capital. The host's contribution is often used as an indicator of his "sincerity" by the donor. Slowness of contribution, on the other hand, is often considered to indicate a lack of interest.

Such an appraisal may be erroneous, however, for the apparent lack of support may be due to the host's sheer lack of resources in the face of multiple demands. Shortages, however, may be due to some conscious restraint exercised by an official with administrative power. For example, it has been argued that Soviet aid to a "neutral" country was for a long time frustrated by the refusal of one minister of the neutral government to cooperate.

Manpower difficulties sometimes arise because of a shortage of trained people. A decision to proceed with the job using whoever is available may result in poor execution. One solution in such cases is to build up the requisite competent administration, which takes time, or to bring in sufficient numbers of outside persons who can perform operational tasks. An early assessment of manpower needs and training potential is thus necessary if later bottlenecks are to be avoided.

The more difficult cases are not those in which there is lack of finance or manpower, but those in which there is a clash of philosophies between donor and recipient. In such situations the attempts of the advisors to get their views accepted may be looked upon as proof of intransigence instead of as a sign of technical competence. The granting of donor funds as a lever for acceptance of the advisor's views may be considered an improper application of the assistance concept. The donor technician's attempts to use the local U.S. mission to influence higher echelons of host government, and thus overrule his technical counterparts, may meet with the traditional bureaucratic response of denigrating "advisors" in general, while creating minor but vexing obstacles in the implementation of the project.

There are many variations in the basic pattern of resource and knowledge shortages. If the host administrators do not know how to solve a problem, even though the problem is recognized, the technicians who act with assurance may, in a sense, enjoy a free hand. This has certain advantages in getting things done speedily.

Competition between a number of potential donor countries may also considerably increase the chances of project success. In the former case the recipient has more room for maneuver because the donor is flexible in order to implement the project.

Fervid insistence by the donor for a project, however, as in the latter case, may endanger its success if the host is only lukewarm.

The role of the advisor is likely to be easily accepted in situations where the competence of the receiver does not rise to the problem at hand. Where there is adequate competence, operational rather than advisory roles become more effective. Similarly, in cases where the experience of the donor country is not relevant to the local problem (often the case in agricultural projects based upon community development), projects may face difficulties. In such cases there is often ignorance on both sides. Here too, if advice is freely offered the response may be negative while an operational role for the donor may be more acceptable.

There are cases in which an agency of the recipient country adopts a program for training skilled manpower without any plans for its immediate use, but the lack of planning for use does not necessarily imply the absence of planning and foresight, for many technical assistance programs deal with only a segment of a more complex undertaking. Agriculture, perhaps more than other activities, highlights the fact that technical assistance has beneficial consequences for the recipient, *only if it is accompanied by a host of parallel developments*. This is so because output cannot be increased merely by demonstrating the feasibility of an improved method of cultivation. The new techniques may not be disseminated; farmers may not be able to get loans for purchasing new implements; the use of fertilizer may require increased use of water, while irrigation facilities may not have been extended in the area; the consumer markets may not stock the goods farmers want, etc. The number of producers involved is generally very large. It is very difficult to reach those involved individually though production may depend ultimately upon their coordinated decisions. Technical assistance is not a simple procedure of give-and-take but a complex exchange and interaction with inherent situations of stress.

Procedural Difficulties

The magnitude, timing, and form of technical assistance have a great bearing on the effectiveness of a program. Failure often revolves around: (1) disagreements over priorities and strategies, (2) recruitment and utilization of personnel, (3) delays in commodity aid, and (4) budget-related procedures. Red-tape delays in getting approvals, etc., are peculiar neither to the United States nor the host administration. These factors become repetitive and tend to appear in some form with great frequency in all administrations.

1. *Disagreements over Priorities or Strategies*

These disagreements may arise at any of three levels. At each they may cause delays and may even cripple the program.

a. *Disagreement between Washington and the local technical mission.* How intense such disagreements can become and the consequent delays are illustrated by a project to help R set up a Mining Assistance Commission.

R has a reasonable mineral resource base. The development and expansion of mining was being directed by the Mineral Research and Exploration Institute (MTA)—a government institution. Because the government had extensive mining operations, the MTA was preoccupied with public sector projects, and it was felt by some in R that the private sector was being neglected. The U.S. Mission supported a proposal for a Mining Assistance Commission. The project was proposed in 1957, and provisions were made for it in assistance programs of AID during the fiscal years (FY) of 1958 and 1959. But on both occasions the project was cancelled, and was not authorized until 1960. One cause of delay was the counter-proposal of the AID Washington office that the Mining Assistance Commission be sponsored by the Mineral Research and Exploration Institute instead of the Union of Chambers of Commerce, which had originally proposed it. During this period, of course, the private sector miners, whom both Washington and the local Mission wanted to help, continued to lack assistance.

b. *Differences in points of view between the USAID and the recipient government.* It is clear that unless the host places a high priority upon the project, the donor's efforts are not likely to be effective.

Two situations should be distinguished in this respect: (1) the donor fails to ascertain whether or not the project "really" figures on the priority list of the recipient. This may happen if the donor "over-sells" a project. The recipient's attitude then is "after all, we are being offered the money, so we might as well take it," and some officials (perhaps those who look forward to visiting the

United States) will tend to be enthusiastic about the project. But the enthusiasm of a few interested officials may not provide the basic capital to complete the project. The fault here lies equally with the donor and the recipient; with the donor for not ascertaining whether the host is or is not really interested in the project; with the recipient (or at least some officials) for putting on a fake show of interest.

(2) An even more serious situation arises when the recipient makes a commitment and later fails to carry out his side of the agreement. Three examples will illustrate this: The Y government seriously defaulted in its contribution for the development of rural institutes. Y had agreed to accept one-half of the recurring and three-fourths of the non-recurring expenses. The provincial states and sponsoring bodies were to accept responsibility for the remainder. The original estimates were the basis on which the technical assistance agreement was concluded; the table indicates the divergence between the original estimate and the actual allocated funds.

	Dollar equivalent of Y currency	
	Non-Recurring	*Recurring*
Original estimates per Institute	$1,365,000	$115,500 *per yr.*
Allocated in Second Plan per Institute	420,000	189,000 *for 5 yrs.*

Two years after the initiation of another project relating to milk supplies for a large city the government indicated that it could not meet its obligations. As a consequence an assisting government also withdrew. The project was saved only because UNICEF stepped in.

The hybrid maize project was "initiated at the strong urging of the government of X, which was aware of the possibility of a major expansion of the fourth most important grain crop in a group of provinces." Yet, delays occurred so frequently and were of such a nature that they could not be attributed to anything except an absence of complete concern on the part of the X government.

Whatever the causes which lead to such situations—failure of the donor to ascertain the priority list of the recipient, misrepresentation of its priorities by the recipient, or the fact that "circumstances changed so that priority had to be given to other projects"

—the result is the failure of technical assistance to be successful. It is as necessary for the recipient to be forthright about his major concerns and to adhere to them insofar as possible as it is for the donor to ascertain what these priorities really are.

c. *Inter-departmental tensions or lack of coordination within the recipient government.* This tension may take either the form of rivalry between departments or levels of government, or it may simply be the failure of one department to maintain the schedule of assignments.

Two examples will illustrate the rivalry constraint. Work on strengthening the Geological Survey of T was delayed by the bureaucracy of T's government because mining was treated as a political matter. The headquarters of the Survey group was shifted time and again, and as an agency it was shunted among three ministries. In P, a project relating to canal operation and maintenance of the large Valley Authority encountered difficulties because, while the Operations Management division of the Authority was looking after the canals, the Agricultural Department was responsible for the operation of certain sublaterals in the system. This made for "some friction in water regulation and control."

With respect to schedules, it appears that the departments which most frequently fail to adhere to the timetable are those responsible for heavy construction work. In A and B the public works departments are notoriously inefficient. The effects of delays in the construction of office buildings may not be harmful to the execution of the technical assistance project if the project is mainly accomplished in the field, e.g., with cooperative credit unions. The project officers can usually make do in any of the existing structures. But the effects of an incomplete building program can be extremely harmful in projects where specialized equipment awaits installation in the new buildings for either production or research purposes.

It should be noted finally, that inter-agency strife within the recipient government may sometimes, though probably not often, be promoted by the actions of several branches of the U.S. Technical Mission itself. In G, administrative decisions by preceding agencies of AID led to the establishment of two overlapping institutions—Agricultural Extension Service and Community Development. This duality resulted in waste and conflict. It was several years before the two were merged. In the meantime, the two institutions had strengthened themselves so that the merger "created many problems in reorganizing, retraining and personnel management."

2. *Recruitment and Placement of Personnel*

The second set of inhibitory factors in assistance programs relates to the recruitment and placement of personnel. Cases where work on a project has been stalled because of inordinate delays in the recruitment and replacement of personnel are not rare.

A full-time technician assigned to a project for assisting the organization of F's Rural Institutes arrived four years after the Institutes began operation. "By that time many structural and operating faults had been institutionalized." This project was initiated in FY 1957. The requests for new technicians were made in 1961!

> U.S. inflexibility prevented quick change of plans; while project elements were being cancelled, the Ministry asked for a technician in rural health and sanitation and hinted at two or three more in teaching training, cooperation, and community development. Upon hearing that our procedures require two-year lead time to produce unanticipated technicians, these informal requests were withdrawn and the project expired.

The Crop Development project in L was initiated in FY 1955. A full-time entomologist was assigned in October, 1956. His contract terminated in October, 1958, but it was not until October, 1960, that a replacement arrived to continue the program. This gap allowed the program to lag.

Aid for the project to assist in the development of Agricultural Credit and Cooperatives in U began in 1960. No American technician had been assigned to the project until April, 1963. The request for an advisor was made in April, 1962. One year later the position had still not been filled. Nevertheless, considerable sums of money were given to the government of U in support of this project.

The decision to assist C in the development of a rich valley was made in 1954. The U.S. Mission had suggested to C that it should provide funds for about eighty man-years of American technical assistance. Neither the provincial state government involved nor the C contractors were interested in such large-scale technical assistance.

> Ultimately it was decided that only four American engineering advisors would be furnished and arrangements were made with the Bureau of Reclamation to recruit these men. Difficulties in recruitment resulted in the shrinkage of the team to three men. . . . The design work was nearing completion by the time the American mechanical and structural engineering advisors arrived at the valley. Consequently, there was little work for them to do strictly as design advisors.

Many examples could be added to this list. But these cases illustrate that delays in recruitment and replacement have been excessive, and that delays have occurred in cases where the requirement needs might have been estimated well in advance, or were known but not acted on by U.S. authorities.

From the viewpoint of the recipient two features lead to recurrent difficulties. The appointments of counterparts are often made on grounds other than competence. One comes across this feature more frequently in countries such as Z and W which have only embryonic civil service corps than in countries with a tradition of civil service. In the former countries, procedures for appointment and dismissal have not been as systematized as in the latter. Even when an agency is reorganized on the counsel of technical advisors, old personnel are retained, and the technical assistance program often never becomes quite effective.

The second source of difficulty is the scarcity of partially-trained persons, or even of persons with a high-school education. In isolated lands, therefore, the selection of counterparts becomes difficult. The few who are available often must be sent abroad for further training, so that they will be capable of running the project themselves. This, while necessary for short periods, intensifies difficulties in the long run. As the scarcity of domestic personnel becomes more widespread, technical advisors are forced to assume routine administrative responsibilities. This retards institutionalization of the program or project while preventing the foreign advisors from concentrating on purely technical aspects. To cite a single example, in a project for organizing agricultural development research in D the effort at organization led to delays so that the proper study and evaluation of data relating to crop experiments could not be carried out.

Almost all reports on projects of extension work in agriculture, dissemination of improved seeds, and cultivation practices, etc., point to the serious handicap of the inadequacy of transport equipment. While money is available for office buildings and personnel, the personnel are immobilized because the transport needs of the programs are underestimated.

3. *Delays in Shipment from the United States to the Recipient*

Extracts from two reports will illustrate the time lags involved and the resultant difficulties due to shipping delays from the United States. In a project to assist E in the development of Mineral Resources and Coal Production, it is reported:

> In planning a project of this kind, considerable importation of specialized equipment and commodities is required. Performance could have been available within reasonable time. There is a minimum lag of two years between the planning and arrival of commodities. There have been instances of changed planning during this period which would have made a somewhat different procurement desirable.

These delays are independent of those caused by the closing of E's borders.

In a project to provide Engineering Services to the Central Water Authority in I:

> The U.S. contributions included commodity purchases for equipment and personnel transportation. Some orders have been eighteen months in delivery. This long delay is very detrimental to progress; for example, five oil field trucks for the drilling crews have been on order for more than eighteen months, and have not been received at time of writing [April, 1963].

Just as the progress of the technical assistance project may be thwarted by delays in supplying equipment, it can also be frustrated by failure of the host to ensure prompt utilization of the equipment. The project to assist J in developing the fisheries industry is instructive because it exposes both the enormous time lags in utilization and also some typical factors accounting for such lags. The project was initiated in FY 1952 and terminated ten years later. The results were not up to initial expectations, and it is bluntly reported that "the primary problem was the non-utilization or under utilization of the equipment supplied." Equipment for a net-making plan was at hand in I for five years but was never used. Apart from the general delays mentioned:

> This activity received a large sum for the purchase of equipment in the initial stages before I ever had an adequate organization or technical personnel that could assimilate or utilize the equipment. Too much equipment was brought in and allowed to sit idle. In general, if AID had spaced the allocation of funds for equipment to coincide with readiness and need, we could have avoided the unsatisfactory situation of having unused equipment on hand.
>
> Three Bull Trawlers: Controlled by a province and are located in a large city. It has been demonstrated that with the use of these vessels, fish catch could be increased considerably. However, they are used only to a limited extent due to pressures from certain sources who virtually control and monopolize the present city fish market. These vested interests are so great that they hamper or limit the pace of development of the country. AID is taking steps to get these vessels shifted from the control of the provincial government to some other location where full use can be effected.

4. *Budgetary Procedures*

Finally, attention must be drawn to delays and difficulties that are often caused by budgetary procedures. Here, as with all other factors, difficulties emanate from the donor as well as from the recipient.

The availability of funds cannot be estimated from the reports. However, the approval of funds is sometimes delayed, and this cools the interest of the donor in seeing that the technical assistance program is speedily implemented.

A somewhat extreme example is provided by a project to assist V develop its forest resources. This project was initiated in FY

1955. Most other prerequisites were available for success such as the strong support of the government, the calibre of the personnel of the Forest Service, "probably the major factor accelerating progress," "educational level, morale and *esprit de corps* were all high. . . . Personnel of the Service were very responsive to technical advice. . . . Such an organization would be an asset to any program." But delays occurred because completion of the Export-Import Loan to the Forest Service took two years. "This delay directly altered time schedules and staffing of the proposed positions. Prevention of this delay was beyond the control of USAID."

For several years work on some projects was handicapped because the AID Mission could not spend U.S. holdings of local (counterpart) currency. A case in point is a project to help Q increase its soil fertility through increased production and utilization of fertilizers. Bureaucratic snags tied up Q's local budget. But it seems that steps have been taken in the recent past to overcome this source of delay.

Budgetary procedures of the recipients often show a high persistence of inefficiency. The case of the V Forest Service mentioned above is instructive. We have noted already that the program had strong support of the host government: "Keen interest has been evidenced from the President on down." And yet from 1955 to 1963 (when the Report was written) a harmfully inefficient budgetary practice was continued. Under the existing budgetary procedures, the Forest Service was required to supply the major portion of its operating expenses from revenues received from the sale of forest products. This in turn discouraged investment of local and foreign capital in forest industries. The high prices did not raise the requisite funds for the Forest Service, so programs for reforestation, soil conservation, range management, etc., suffered. Nevertheless, the forestry budget was not merged with general revenues. The reason for this may well have been a reluctance to devote additional resources to forestry. One may surmise that, in spite of the enthusiasm, forest development was not high on the V priority list.

Piecemeal budgeting is another deficiency which has led to difficulties in the administration procedures of recipients. One of the reasons for delays in the hybrid-maize development project in a province of U referred to above was that each year budgets were sanctioned for approximately twenty different schemes, yet all the schemes had the same objective. Piecemeal budgeting complicated financial support and made steady overall progress impossible. Confusions and delays are apparent at all levels.

These examples show that deficient budgetary procedures do sometimes lead to difficulties and delays. But the examination of project reports indicates that they are usually *not* so significant as the other factors.

Illustrative Cases

The technical assistance cases discussed in this section are divided into five groups, (1) Education, (2) Vocational adult training, (3) Administrative Cases, (4) Agricultural and Resource Development.

1. *Education*

In this group we have included educational projects in which the basic problem is centered around two questions: Can technical assistance be effective if the educational system being developed by the receiving country is not patterned after American institutions? Can an individual program operating under an American system be isolated from the country's other programs which are based upon premises differing from the American system?

A description of cases is given below with a discussion of the particularly significant factors.

The project for assisting the Engineering College of M University has been described as a failure by the reporting officer in the following words:

> Broadly speaking, this project has been expensive but has not been successful in the attainment of the non-physical objectives which were formulated for it. Physical facilities have been expanded . . . [but] expectations with respect to changes in the institutional factors pertaining to such a structure have remained unfulfilled. . . . The failure of this project . . . is not likely to seriously affect national development . . . [but] if this project had been successful the university would have gained

in its ability to play a constructive role in M's industrial . . . development.

The Engineering College was started in 1951 under a foreign aid program with a seventeen-man faculty "all trained in England." Still the facilities were not adequate for expanding needs, and in 1958 the government of M requested assistance from the U.S. Mission for further development of the college. An American agricultural college was awarded a contract to assist the college.

The American advisory team failed in its attempt to revise the curriculum and introduce different administrative methods because

> interest within the University . . . is focused largely, if not exclusively, on financial and physical assistance, not on technical advice.

The reason for this is traced to

> the built-in institutional hegemony of the British over the professional education system. . . . The U.S. Agricultural staff were triply handicapped; they were not British trained, and were not, therefore, fully qualified professionally in the eyes of some of their counterparts; they were not from Harvard or M.I.T. . . . which would have helped to overcome the first "handicap," and they did not have a doctoral degree in all cases . . . which might again have overcome their "deficiencies" in other respects.

The conclusion is that

> a more careful analysis of sociological and cultural factors should have preceded the formulation of the project.

However, M was able to construct a campus for two thousand students and equip laboratories without having to introduce an American agricultural college in a university which was developed and patterned after the University of London.

The objective of changing the pattern of education failed in the case of M, but it is reported to have been successful in K at the K University. In 1958 it was proposed to make a medical center a part of K University. The contract was awarded to an American university which carried out a comprehensive two-year survey.

The objective was to change from limited "participation in medical care standards . . . towards an enlarged vision of the introduction of American methods of medical education." This was considered necessary because medical education in K had been patterned after the "traditional French system" which had not kept up with the times. The major opposition to the proposed changes came from "a small but influential minority representing those trained in the earlier European tradition." Delays in implementation were caused by K's inability to fill such vital positions in the university's top-level administration as provost and executive secretary with men oriented toward American educational systems. Support, however, came from "a handful of young U.S. trained physicians." Diplomatic access to the head of state and "pressures exerted at the time of development or extension of a contract" succeeded in bringing about the desired changes. The shift to American methods in the administration of the medical school

> led to changes in the organization and administration of the whole university set-up at the Medical College on the grounds that a western-type medical school could function only within the framework of a western-oriented university. This . . . posed some exceedingly difficult transitional problems. . . . Only the personal interest of the Head of State made possible the emergence of K University in its present form.

The report is very optimistic concerning the possible effects of the project on K's educational system as a whole:

> Measured in terms of the resistance engendered . . . the success of this project may have considerable significance . . . in altering educational patterns . . . in other areas.

The attempt to pattern the AA Institute of Technology after vocational rather than engineering education met with opposition from UNESCO which had provided technical assistance during the first two years of the project. When U.S. technicians arrived (prior to 1959), disputes regarding objectives led to the establishment of a separate Polytechnic Institute by UNESCO on the same campus. The dispute finally resulted in the removal of the U.S.-supported institute to a different site. The reporting officer comments:

The experience . . . is illustrative of problems of competing foreign educational philosophies in a developing country . . . the European-oriented UN technicians sought to train practical engineers . . . who on the basis of several weeks of pedagogical training were expected to qualify as trade and industrial teachers. . . . In spite of the signed project agreements . . . the Institute gradually changed its character from a teacher training institution to an engineering school.

The U.S. technicians who arrived in 1959 insisted that "original objectives be restored" and that students be trained as vocational teachers with emphasis on shop training and not as practical engineers. This was opposed by AA education officials who pressed for the "inclusion of engineering content in the curriculum leading to M.S. degree in engineering [saying that] . . . only two or three weeks of pedagogy were necessary to prepare an engineer to teach." As no agreement was reached, the U.N. decided to establish an independent Polytechnic Institute for the training of engineers. The report avers:

Logic might have dictated a compromise in favor of an engineering degree . . . with a modified curriculum . . . with somewhat more American-type pedagogy . . . [but] the Education Division tenaciously insisted upon adhering to the prior agreement,

arguing that the salaries of shop teachers were half those of engineers and if the students were given engineering degrees none would become a teacher.

A resolution of the problem came after three years of administrative infighting. The AA government doubled teachers' salaries while the U.S. Mission agreed to reduce the course of Bachelor of Vocational Education from four to three years so that a graduate could become an engineer with one additional year of training. The U.S.-supported institute was removed from its original site, to get away from the

engineering influence . . . of the UN sponsored Polytechnic institute . . . [leaving] the broader issue [of choice] . . . between European and American inspired systems an active problem for AA educators (still to resolve).

The situation is not always as critical as the above descriptions may suggest. Where technical assistance has functioned within an existing operational setup, or, alternatively, where it has been comprehensive enough to cover all related fields, philosophical (cultural) difficulties have not arisen. Thus, in the case of an Institute of Technology in YY, it seems that no one was aware of a clash of philosophies. We are told that in 1960 the President of the United States assented to the act for the establishment of the institute "in the pattern of U.S. educational methods suitably adapted to country needs."

The U.S. Mission supported a team of six engineering professors assembled by the American Society for Engineering Education. The team visited existing institutes and industries for six weeks and prepared an outline of a proposal. Both the recipients and the Americans "wanted it to be a truly high-level institution of the Massachusetts Institute of Technology type." A team from MIT supported the idea.

As MIT could not undertake the project alone, nine universities collaborated to form a consortium. The United States has made a commitment for 105 man-years of technicians, one-year visits of ninety participants to the United States, equipment worth $4.2 million and construction to cost $4 million. The director of the institute is reported to be "one of the most competent and dynamic among local administrators"; the United States relaxed mandatory two-year assignment technicians, enabling shorter visits of men of high quality, and the institute is said to give promise of becoming "the, or at least one of the four, top institutes of technology in the country." When fully operating it will have 1600 undergraduate and 400 post-graduate students.

A crash program for more advanced training of engineering teachers was a similar success. The government made arrangements through UNESCO to get higher training for 231 teachers in the United States, Germany, Czechoslovakia, France, and the USSR. The rapid expansion of engineering institutes, however, required a larger number of teachers. The U.S. Mission offered training for 300 participants. Between 1958 and 1961 a total of 235 masters degree candidates and 37 doctoral candidates returned after completion of their degrees.

"After the first year's training it was quite common for participants to earn top marks. More than a few earned straight A records."

A similar educational development is reported in connection with the establishment of the Teachers Training Institute in a government university in GG. At the very outset

> it was recognized that GG could not borrow any one system of education from abroad. . . . All educational systems have benefited . . . by the adoption of elements . . . [from] outside the confines of [their] borders. . . . This project sought to build on the sound foundations already established.

The contract was awarded to a midwestern university, but cooperative arrangements were worked out with UNESCO, another American university, and an interested foundation. The Mission Director's appraisal is that

> thorough preparation for getting the project underway . . . firm government policy . . . competent and timely staffing on both the U.S. and GG sides, timely availability of P.L.480 funds . . . is paying off in expeditious implementation that gives reason to expect outstanding results. . . . [The project] has maintained sustained interest and pride of association preventing the normal discouragements.

The case of primary education in isolated TT is interesting because there was neither conflict nor an existing structure to build upon. In 1951 there were only 100 students of the primary school-age group. Since 1954, when the U.S. Mission agreed to provide assistance, the number of schools has risen to 4000 and the number of students to 205,000!

The project has tended to become all-inclusive: the provision of equipment, preparation of teaching materials, training of teachers, and construction of buildings have been integrated. As a result, not only quantitative progress has taken place but also the quality of education has improved. "The curriculum has adopted newer techniques . . . materials known to us in the West have been introduced and are being utilized." Although there was some delay in starting the Educational Materials Project since the decision was made in 1959, rapid progress has been reported. A Writers Division, under the direction of a man who studied in the United States, was established to prepare textbooks. A Production and Distribution Center will ensure that "educational materials written in their own language" will be available to all schools on a uniform basis.

In summary we may observe that:

(1) The "failure" in the case of M University Engineering College or the AA Institute of Technology was not a failure of technical assistance. It was neither directly nor entirely caused by social and cultural factors, though these are mentioned repeatedly in the reports. In both situations the U.S. advisors were opposed by other technical experts whose views were accepted by the host country. The British *vs.* the United States view seems to be a major issue, although the attachment of M to a British ideal may be viewed as a cultural attachment. In both cases unsuccessful attempts which were made to force the situation led to frustration.

(2) The "success" in the case of K University was achieved by enlisting the personal support of the head of state. It may become permanent if aid is continued on a substantial scale for a considerable period of time. If this does not happen, then the small group of dedicated U.S.-oriented educationists may still be swamped by the European-oriented educationists who seem to control the K Ministry of Education. The dispute itself is obviously unreal because a European-oriented educational system does not necessarily stop development, and is not by nature inferior to the U.S. system. The cultural differences are between the two groups of advisors. K presumably is willing to accept either view within limits.

(3) That assistance can be effective in education without a wholesale change in educational structure is shown by the cases from GG and YY. The U.S. teams concentrated on developing technical competence and providing equipment, leaving the question of curriculum and objectives for final decisions with the recipient country.

(4) The TT case shows that where local manpower is not available and development has not yet taken place, a wholesale import of educational ideas from abroad is both desirable and necessary.

2. *Vocational and Adult Training*

This group of projects is characterized by three main features as regards objectives, (1) establishing an organization where none has existed before, (2) fashioning the organization into working form so that it can continue on its own power, and (3) assuring that the organization is integrated into the environment, so that the training and skills are utilized and not wasted.

The literacy level of adults and the training of nurses, mechanics, or hotel staff are not as exciting as the issues which occupied our attention in the preceding section, but they are a part of the development of the technology of a country.

In adult training the needs and aims are easily usually discernible and have a readily definable content. As a result, such mundane administrative problems as the selection of people, the fixing of salaries, the procurement of material, etc., take on relatively great significance. The regular educational programs have to compete for support with the older programs, which are often short of funds for expansion. The new activity then becomes highly dependent upon external assistance until its social role is well recognized (legitimated).

The establishment of a hotel school in DD provides a good example of a case where a project had been shelved for years after studies by French and Belgian tourism experts, because the project was considered "beyond the capabilities of the DD economy."

The U.S. Mission came into the picture after a chance mention of the fact that, through French and Belgian assistance, the Ministry of Education had a trained staff but still needed financial aid. Excepting one-fourth of the salary of one technician for twelve months, no dollar expenditure was involved, but local currency from counterpart funds was provided. The school produced fifty-nine short-course graduates in the first year and had an enrollment of ninety for a three-year course.

Two difficulties were encountered. First, the students were quite eager to learn management and bookkeeping techniques. They were, however, reluctant at first to consider food preparation and service as a career because these areas of work had been "traditionally delegated to the uneducated." The award of the "highly valued lycee diploma upon graduation" and greater financial awards brought about noticeable change in this attitude."

The second difficulty was more general and is summarized in the following words:

> The program is inhibited by the lack of adequate administrative skills or hotel experience among the Ministry of Education persons responsible for the establishment of the School. They are certainly sincere . . . but . . . they are bound by traditional educational and administrational concepts and lack of specialized training. Examples of the problem . . . are: reluctance to purchase luxury foods for the kitchen class; reluctance to pay salaries adequate for the employment of specialized personnel . . . in spite of the fact that the counterpart funds . . . could be expanded without the extreme restrictions that the [Education Ministry] budget imposes.

> It is worthwhile to note . . . that without freedom to use counterpart budget flexibility, the hotel school could not have been opened.

The report is optimistic concerning the possibility of employing the graduates of the school when tourism, and with it the hotel services, expands.

Somewhat similar is the case of two nursing schools, one in MM, the other in OO, though there is one difference: both projects are parts of a larger national health program and as such did not have to assert themselves to the same extent as did the hotel school.

The College of Nursing in OO was established in 1955 to train nurses and nursing supervisors who had already received basic training in nursing schools. The Nursing Education Advisors were directly involved because "their effectiveness . . . has been enhanced by the fact that they have not been limited to a strictly advisory capacity." The big issue was money, since the problem "which has impeded progress centers around one major item, namely, budget."

The School of Nursing in MM was established in 1958 to provide three-year advanced courses in nursing. Here also it was necessary "for advisors to function in an operational capacity . . . [they], through necessity, taught in English [until] in March 1961 the MM faculty decided that teaching must be done in [the native language]." The acceptance of nursing as a profession of Muslim girls is one of the culture obstacles mentioned in the Reports, although it appears that trainees are available. The barrier seems to be traditional rather than religious, but either is a cultural consideration. Male nurses do not seem to have been considered.

The question of employment of trained personnel is illustrated very well by two projects in WW. In the case of the Technical Training Centers for Construction Equipment Maintenance, the number of centers was increased from two to four and utilization of trained personnel is very high. In the case of Hot Line Maintenance (electrical lines), the number of training centers was reduced from two to one even before the termination of the assistance, and the utilization of trained personnel has been low. First we shall discuss the failure.

In 1956 the Central Power and Water Commission (CPWC) requested U.S. assistance for the establishment of centers to train hot line maintenance crews as a result of "intensive missionary program and promotional efforts" of a foreign expert who explained to the CPWC senior engineers the importance of uninterrupted power supply and the U.S. and Canadian practices of hot line maintenance. By 1962 when the project ended, 190 persons had been trained for six months each, forming 42 possible crews; 14 sets of tools had been provided by AID, and 7 were purchased by local authorities. However, it was found that only 7 sets and 24 trainees were in full use while 9 sets with 36 persons were only occasionally used in hot line maintenance. High insurance which was necessary to get crews and instructors working on hot lines was not provided in all cases. Explaining the situation, the government of WW put forth the view that

> the adoption of hot line maintenance works . . . will effect considerable improvement [but its] systematic implementation . . . cannot be achieved in a matter of a few years . . . in all the States [because] several hundred batches of the trained crews and an equal number of hot line tools will be required even to cover the important sections of the transmission systems in this country.

Of two training centers opened in 1958 one was closed in 1961 and only one continues to operate. The Report evaluates the project in the following terms:

> Most of the difficulties encountered in connection with this project stemmed almost directly from a lack of real concern on the part of the Government operating officials. . . . The Mission was unrealistically optimistic in expecting that State Electricity boards and other electric power agencies would adopt hot line maintenance immediately after trained men and equipment became available. Bureaucratic inertia in the public power agencies is great. . . . Though progress is slower . . . it probably is as good as should have been expected. . . . Many (perhaps most) of the Senior engineers of the State Electricity Boards . . . are "sold" on [hot line maintenance] but they are slow in making their influence felt.

An interesting side light on inter-governmental relations is provided by the following description of a conference called to review the situation.

> When the Mission expressed its opinion that utilization had been "extremely poor," government officials reviewed the situation in various States in an attempt to show that utilization . . . was not as poor as represented by this mission. . . . However, personal knowledge of the situation served to discolor the picture painted by CPWC . . . on which the chief government official suggested . . . inspection . . . to assess the situation . . . and make sure that proper facilities were available . . . [to introduce hot line maintenance].
>
> Following this meeting, unfriendly tone of which is obvious, the Training Center was closed and its staff assigned for inspection to ascertain if facilities for the introduction of hot line maintenance did in fact exist.

In contrast to the above case, we get the following report on utilization of the construction equipment maintenance personnel trained at the Technical Training Centers.

> Since inauguration of this project 490 trainees have graduated. . . . All have been employed immediately. . . . The last class of 39 . . . received 115 job offers. . . . The Chief Engineer of

National Projects Construction Corporation . . . has offered to take the entire class to graduate . . . in July 1963.

The government agency involved is once again the CPWC. The project succeeded even though the first contractor selected by the AID had had no experience with the work and had to be dropped in 1957 after two years of "disappointing performance." A new contractor was selected.

> This project after a slow start and a disappointing effort by the first contractor, has become a highly successful example of the benefits to be gained from competent U.S. technical assistance. . . . The rate of progress has been fully compatible with the original expectations. . . . The experience . . . will facilitate . . . transition to [recipient] operation . . . and contribute to the Government of WW's capability of establishing other new schools.

The cases we have discussed thus far in this section deal with action on a rather limited scale, namely the training of a few persons in particular skills. A different kind of problem arises when the impact of the program is on a large number of people. In such cases organizational effectiveness becomes the essence of success.

In this regard we shall deal with two labor-training projects organized through trade union and industry and two adult literacy and training projects instituted within the existing framework of the army.

The major problem in each case was to convert an existing organization to a new kind of activity, and then to evoke support for its implementation. Once adopted, all four projects seemed to have moved with already considerable speed even though one, the literacy and adult education program in PP, was pulled and dragged in a tug-of-war between the Defense and the Education ministries until 1962, when the army and civilian programs were merged.

The training of labor and labor leaders in trade union work in PP provides an interesting example of organizational adjustment because of its obvious political overtones. The project was started in 1954 for the development of "sound trade unions and better labor management relations . . . [through] a labor education program." It was administered through the Employment Service of the Labor Ministry; 90,000 workers participated in lectures and film presentations during lunch hour and "free time provided by the employers"; 5000 trade union officials participated in weekend and evening seminars in which labor laws were explained.

Following the change in government in 1960, steps were taken to put the program in the hands of PP. This was done in 1962. As to accomplishments it is reported:

> Prior . . . to this project European Democratic Socialists exerted a degree of influence on the thinking of the leaders. . . . Our approach emphasizes . . . pragmatic rather than ideological lines. . . . We emphasize bread and butter issues, i.e., rate of pay, bonus, and working conditions. This has counteracted to some extent the Europeans' political approach. [They] are now more interested in collective bargaining, [and] grievance procedure[s].

No major difficulties are mentioned in the execution of the project except for some delay in the appointment by the Union of six regional directors. The political maneuvering of the director of research, who "spent most of his time unsuccessfully proselytizing for the left-wing Workers' party," did provide an obstacle. He finally had to be replaced by the leaders of the PP Trade Union.

A similar agreement concerning objectives was present in the case of an Inplant Training project in FF. The difficulties mentioned in implementation are:

> the low status—almost scorn—of the manual worker, tendency to think of all training as academic, and difficulty to get at facts due to a general reluctance to speak out because it is considered impolite to say anything critical.

But as regards performance of the FF counterparts we told that

> for the most part it would be hard to find a harder-working, more dedicated and sincere group of people. In spite of the fact that they had very little or no background in the field of industrial training, the degree to which they have become proficient in this field is outstanding. In a few instances it is little short of amazing.

The project succeeded in significant ways, and in three years over 11,000 workers were trained, four district training offices were established, training schemes for 132 industrial establishments were prepared, of which 116 were already in operation by 1962. Two interesting features of the project may be noted here: It did not start with a comprehensive manpower-need survey. Instead, it proceeded with short inquiries "to establish generally accepted facts and conditions." A national survey would have caused "delays during which the situation could rapidly change." The Employment Service of the Ministry of Labor and the Chamber of Commerce and Industry joined in canvassing nearly one hundred major plants "to determine the interest of their management of training programs and their willingness to participate in them."

The conditions were not so favorable, however, when an attempt was made to introduce vocational training for conscripts in the NN Army. The U.S. Military Assistance Advisory Group (MAAG) felt that it could not participate unless "the program was clearly an adjunct of military training," while the initial response of the NN military authorities was negative since they believed that

> civilian type training . . . would detract from essential military training and . . . maximum combat preparedness. The maximum obtainable concession . . . was that off-duty and post-conscript time of NN military personnel . . . outside the premises of military installation, might be made available.

Three times each year the military conscripted 50,000 men, 90 per cent of whom were illiterate. In 1959 the government of NN proposed to set up a Vocational Training Institute where conscripts could be sent after their military training. The NN government requested the U.S. Mission to provide $3.5 million in assistance. The AID offered to consider the proposal

> provided these centers were allocated space in existing military installations outside [a major city] and the training was part of the NN Army's program for its two-year conscripts.

We are told that "this *tache* and the discussions which ensued helped during 1960 and 1961 . . . [to gather] considerable support for the idea of civic action among a number of officers in the NN Army and the MAAG," which led to an agreement between AID,

MAAG, NN Army, and the Planning Organization in 1962. The project has progressed on schedule, and vocational teachers have been trained despite the "language barrier and difficulty of communication." It is expected that this project will train 7,200 conscripts in nine skills annually. Three-month courses were contemplated in metal-working, woodworking, plumbing, masonry, electricity, mechanics, welding, and leather and shoe repair.

Two weaknesses are mentioned in connection with the project: there is a "need to find a way to provide each man who completes the course with a basic kit of tools for his trade," and to include "instruction in improved agricultural techniques." A third, of course, is to provide work for the trained people.

A literacy and adult education program, however, was easier to introduce by the WF Forces because the army immediately saw that an effective, modern army could not be developed with half of the conscripts illiterate. It was simply necessary to allocate some time for the education of the captive audience. Under the program 207,000 recruits were given a basic four months literacy-training course, and between 50,000 and 55,000 are to be trained each year. Training for adult education was provided by 4200 primary school teachers who were doing their military service.

3. *Administrative Cases*

The cases that we have discussed so far are administrative in the general area of education. The cases are almost wholly within the orbit of governmental action and are concerned with the application of known techniques to known problems.

We shall now examine four cases of airport facilities development, one case of an airline operation, and five cases of the improvement of existing services. These cases also involve administration, but the technical levels differ in being more specialized than those of education. Also, each case has an individual goal different in nature from the others.

The first case concerns the development of ground aviation facilities. It illustrates the variety of impediments which can burden an organization, even when problems relating to finance and technically qualified manpower are not onerous.

The project was started in 1955 to help develop airport facilities in AB and to provide training to the personnel of the Directorate-

General of Civil Aviation (DGCA). U.S. assistance was provided through a Civil Aviation Assistance Group (CAAG) assigned by the U.S. Federal Aviation Agency (FAA).

The project was suspended in the spring of 1958 because of AB's lack of cooperation. It was reactivated in December, 1958, and since then has made very satisfactory progress. With regard to funds, the government of AB "fully supported the project financially," while on the U.S. side the only financial difficulties encountered were: the relocation of 1958 funds in FY 1959. Also, in FY 1960 AID transferred $2 million in favor of "other fiscal needs of that particular time." This necessitated a Development Loans Fund (DLF) loan which took two years to negotiate.

> The manpower situation was favorable. On the country side the DGCA and predecessor agencies had excellent technical talent . . . though too few in number to fully cope . . . with daily operations and at the same time with the development program. A favorable factor for the latter part of the project has been determination to do both.

while on the U.S. side the CAAG was staffed by

> personnel having sound technical competence . . . and broad background extending well beyond the technical aspects of the project.

The first three years of the project were disappointing. The director general of Civil Aviation was a "third country national," (presumably British), who was "averse to United States systems, methods and men." He was replaced by an AB national who had no aviation experience. The AB project director was constantly checked "by an opposing faction in the internal strife of the Department." The frustration caused by this situation led to the suspension of the assistance in 1958,

> upon which the AB government gave vent to considerable acrimony . . . [but this] had the salutory effect of making it aware of the U.S.'s expecting responsive compliance with the Project Agreement.

The project was reactivated after the military change in government. A reconstituted CAAG arrived in spring of 1959, while the

DGCA was placed under the commander-in-chief of the Air Force. The importance of the project to AB is clear from this administrative gambit. Since that time no major difficulties arose in the implementation of the program. Routine difficulties are mentioned in the staffing of the CAAG where "some delays in filling positions . . . had an adverse effect" and there were delays in the delivery of equipment.

> Much of the specialized equipment takes from eighteen months to over two years between order and delivery. Adding to this time consumed has been the practice of accumulating requisitions to avail of bulk prices . . . some more or less shelf items taking three years to delivery. . . . Suspension of the project, non-availability of funds and slow delivery resulted in the amassing of component parts which did not constitute complete facilities.

These difficulties, however, did not affect the rate of progress which kept to schedule except for a one year's delay due to the suspension of the project. The reasons for success are mentioned as

> frequently held CAAG/DGA progress meetings at working level and higher . . . led to understanding between persons concerned. . . . The practice of clearing all pertinent matters with the DGCA, whether or not their concurrence was required, tended to create a will to cooperate. . . . The CAAG made clear that civil action . . . [was] the government's responsibility [and] . . . maintained a position avoiding omniscient or superior attitudes in recognition of AB's prerogatives and capabilities. . . . [It recognized that] disclosures of deficiencies . . . or seemingly undue reliance on foreign assistance may well affect DGCA officials' and employees' sensibilities if not their careers [and] therefore proceeded on the premise that accomplishment would be greater if CAAG disregarded immediate credit due the Group. . . . Improvements and corrective measures devised by CAAG were first offered informally to the DGCA official responsible for the function. This approach was appreciated and almost always led to implementing action by the official concerned. In the few cases where this approach failed, action was taken in accord with contractual obligations.

This approach helped overcome the feelings left over from the days of "somewhat anti-American and uncooperative leadership" in AB's Civil Aviation Department prior to 1958.

A similar project in GF encountered problems which differed from those in AB. In AB, technical competence was available, and inactivity was the result of administrative disagreements in the Aviation Department. In GF, on the other hand, there was almost a vacuum as far as technical manpower was concerned. The project was bogged down in rivalry and conflict between the fifteen members of the International Civil Aviation Organization (ICAO) advisory team and the U.S. advisors, which led to a situation in which "the GF technician . . . never knew, for sure, whom he should approach for advice."

Between 1952 and 1957, AID had relied on the ICAO team to give technical assistance for purchase of equipment and for the training of personnel. In 1957 the first member of the FAA arrived to form the U.S. Civil Aviation Assistance Group (CAAG). The mission director describes the subsequent relationship as follows:

> By mutual agreement, the primary leadership role . . . had been exercised by the ICAO Mission with the FAA team playing a secondary role. . . . The FAA team, with expanded responsibilities for a regional project, succeeded in reversing their position (in 1962) *vis-à-vis* ICAO . . . and . . . are now *de facto* playing the primary role.

From the reports of the Technical Division, however, it is obvious that the CAAG never accepted a "secondary role." The report of the Technical Division considers as one of the major inhibiting factors

> the early reliance by AID (1952–1957) on the ICAO team for technical advice rather than on U.S. technicians [and later] a very strong tendency by the DGCA and the ICAO team to consider CAAG as simply a source of men and materials.

With the reduction of the ICAO team from fifteen to three members and with a clear division of responsibility which has established the position of the CAAG as advisor for communication and navigation aid, progress would have been greater.

It is evident at this time that better response at higher levels of the government of GF would have been experienced had there been a greater understanding by GF's government officials of the need for U.S. assistance and advice *and* commodities rather than the last only.

Despite the inability of the GF government to recognize the "true advisors," and conflict within the U.S. Mission concerning the respective roles of the ICAO and the CAAG teams, the physical facilities have been installed and personnel trained so that

a basic organizational framework . . . exists and constitutes a capability to maintain the air navigational aids network with a minimum of outside assistance.

We may end this case with an interesting description of one of the accelerating factors mentioned in the Report.

Certain characteristics of the GF national average have been found to be encouraging in the pursuit of the project objective. The U.S. technicians have found that most of the counterparts . . . are intensely subjective minded: if the counterpart can perform work which permits him to feel that he is bettering himself, or if he can work at something which he considers his own, he performs in a very enthusiastic manner. . . . During equipment installation periods [they] readily agreed to work more than eight hours a day rather than the usual 5–½ or 6.

The other two projects of airport facilities development in PL and TO also have moved ahead after certain initial clarifications had been worked out. In PL the major obstacle was its change in national status which required renegotiation of the agreement. An ICAO school provided basic training while advance training and new installations were the responsibility of CAAG.

The TO project illustrates a different kind of problem. The CAAG technicians in this case were supported by "counterparts at all levels which made it possible to deal directly with responsible officials," while top-level Civil Aviation officials "understood and appreciated the technical scope and complexity of the problems." In spite of these favorable factors, the Civil Aviation Department, in common with other TO agencies, has undertaken an expansion program

> which is in fact beyond the capability of the organization to complete within the scheduled time. . . . [It has to make] efforts on a priority basis . . . [because of] insufficient technical capability to carry out all elements of the project concurrently.

Recognizing the shortage of technical manpower, the project carried out a crash training program. Of sixty-five persons trained in three years, sixty-two are on the job (two were lost because they did not return, and one was sent out as an advisor to another country by the government). The communication and navigation systems were expected to take one year's preparation, but a special difficulty arose with respect to maintenance because of a failure on the part of the Civil Aviation Department to "make long-range detailed plans for replacement of worn and damaged parts."

> There is a tendency to replace an expensive facility rather than to repair it [or to request] financial assistance to procure spare parts. [This] has been discouraged [because] granting funds for procurement of spare parts to repair the equipment would in no way resolve the basic spare parts problem,

especially when the government had committed itself to provide funds for maintenance and repair of equipment.

We may note that in all four cases the program has been able to achieve its basic objective—the creation of operational airport facilities and trained technical manpower. There were difficulties in delivery of equipment on time and in maintaining full-scale advisory services. Both sides, however, gave high priority to the projects, and financial difficulties were minimal. Still in one case internal strife within the Civil Aviation Department, in another strife between the ICAO and U.S. technicians, in a third political separation of the country, and in the fourth the desire for rapid expansion, caused delays in implementation.

The question naturally arises: were these delays avoidable? Most delays are avoidable from hindsight, but they may not have been avoidable for the people actually involved in the actions. We can see, however, from the AB case, that a situation in which competent and sympathetic leadership is lacking in a ministry or department, the project can be advanced only through the adoption of extraordinary tactics. One has to be sure that such a situation exists before using such extreme tactics as placing an essentially civilian function under the military.

The GF case shows that where funds are provided by the United States, but advice is given by an independent technical agency, an inherently unstable situation is created. (A similar problem existed in the Institute of Technology case discussed earlier.) The host country is then unable to make a decision (even if it had the competence to do so) until it is sure how it is going to gain or lose by choosing one rather than another position. The DGCA in GF decided to give full support to the CAAG only when regional funds made it necessary to choose between CAAG and the IACO's technical assistance team.

The TO case illustrates the difficulties in getting a comprehensive program introduced when the possibility of aid prompts the host government to make obviously unwise decisions in favor of over-expansion at the cost of not making provisions for repairs and maintenance. To what extent this was motivated by an inability to plan and to what extent it was a tactical measure for getting additional funds is difficult to assess.

The development of an international airlines between 1955 and 1962 shows how, after an initial period of uncertain relationship, the recipient country (AB) succeeded in full utilization of the technical personnel made available to it. The contract was awarded to Pan American Airways (PAA) for the whole period.

> For the first nine months there was high level opposition to the advisory team within the airline. A lack of cooperation characterized the early years of the contract. This was due not only to overt opposition but to personality differences among both AB nationals and Americans. It was only natural for the Americans to aspire to quick progress and it was also natural for the AB nationals to react with caution, not being sure of where they were being led. . . . The reluctance of AB airline personnel and departments to adopt the recommendations of the Advisory Team emerged as a retarding factor in

the early stages of the project. . . . There [was] a large turnover of the PAA technicians as a result of resignations because of the lack of cooperation and receptivity on the part of the AB nationals [and] due to delays in the delivering of project commodities which did not begin to arrive until 1957 [thus preventing] them from performing with reasonable effectiveness.

At the outset, the exact status of the PAA technicians was confused. These technicians were

in an advisory capacity but AB Airlines, through misunderstanding, sought to give them operational responsibilities. [Also] in case of each replacement [of an advisor] it required considerable time, quite generally at the start, for the PAA technicians to demonstrate their competence and gain AB Airline's confidence.

The contract provided for the assignment to the Airline of thirty-one technicians to act as "advisors and deputies to supervisory personnel." These services accounted for the bulk of the expenditures, $4.095 million, compared to $0.534 million, on commodities for training purposes, while participant training cost only $0.72 million. The emphasis was upon the development of training facilities within the country.

In 1961–62 . . . 189 courses were conducted and several foreign airlines took advantage of AB Airline's schooling including nationals from Europe and Asia.

The project was phased out in 1962. By this time the AB Airline had matured from

a local operation . . . to a full-fledged airline operating with the most modern equipment over international routes and in competition with the older and more experienced airlines. In 1962 it was already earning 87 per cent of its foreign exchange requirements and its balance-sheet showed a favorable balance of the equivalent of almost a million dollars after adjustment of losses of the earlier years. It set a record of daily utilization of 11.0 hours on Boeing B–720; 7.44 hours on Lockheed L–1049 and 8.34 hours on Viscount V–815. This record and the airline's schedule regularity are acknowledged as among the best in the industry.

In summary we are told that

> to define the actual effect of PAA's work would be nearly impossible. AB Airline was making progress prior to the employment of PAA and no doubt would have attained a portion of the goal without any help. . . . [However] the team was deeply involved in AB Airline operations taking major actions, reviewing current problems and assigning responsibility for their solution. The end result of the cooperative effort . . . was the attainment of the goal.

We now turn to a different kind of administrative case in which improved effectiveness of a governmental agency was the major objective. The most interesting case is that of the Central Statistical Office (CSO) in QY where the avowed objective was nothing short of creating a miniature U.S. Census Bureau. The resources needed, however, included twenty-eight man-years of technical advice over a period of twelve years. A large gap continued to exist in the availability of technical personnel and the demand for it, so much so that

> each Statistical Advisor . . . ended up as Acting Director . . . of CSO with all the administrative and program complications . . . [until] in Spring of 1958 AID announced that . . . no further assistance [would be] given . . . until [the appointment of] a qualified [nationals].

Out of thirty-nine participants sent abroad (twenty-six in the U.S. and thirteen under U.N. and other assistance) only half returned to the CSO, while the others were "diverted to other (even though often important) assignments." A director-general was appointed in 1958, but "serious staff shortage" has continued. The report wistfully remarks that

> in retrospect it appears that the U.S. might have recognized the dimensions of the problems . . . at least five years earlier and moved with more extensive technical advice, more physical aid to struggling research and training institutions and more opportunities to train local statisticians at home and abroad.

Considerations of finance and manpower do not seem to have affected the U.S. AID effort in the development of police services in LE and UT. Both services were handicapped by lack of transport and modern communication facilities and out-of-date record keeping and procedural systems. In both countries only cities were involved since the rural areas were controlled by the armies.

In LE the project was started in 1955. With little increase in size (21,196 in 1962, 26,000 in 1956) or jurisdiction (156 cities with populations of 5000 and over in 1952, 153 cities in 1956), efforts were concentrated upon the training of men and the supplying of equipment. By 1962, 123 of the cities had been linked by AM radio to the capital; mobile and base stations were established; 129 trainees were sent to the United States; 1125 completed three-year officers' courses; 3519 took in-service training; and 4,646 patrolmen were given patrolmen's courses. The project is considered a success.

In UT, too, a communication network was established, and the UT National Police were well-equipped. A political revolution, however, is reported to have lowered the morale because the UT police were "widely believed to be an instrument of the party in power."

An example of saturation aid in a country with rudimentary administrative services is provided by the contract given to the Public Administration Service (PAS) in RG. A contingent of nine advisors has been maintained there since 1957. It has concentrated its work in the Finance Ministry trying to work out and implement specific schemes in budgeting, accounting, revenue and income tax, customs, supply, personnel, etc. The progress "as a whole has exceeded expectations."

It does not follow, however, that it is always necessary to have a large contingent of advisors in order to bring about change. The case of State Supply Office (DMO) in RY provides a good illustration. The DMO had a staff of about 550 in the supply division and 1000 in the printing division. It made annual purchases worth $110 million (half of it in foreign exchange). The lack of familiarity with modern management practices and competent staff services, over-centralized administration, the overstaffing in some key departments, crowded office conditions, and lack of technical knowledge at top levels hindered effective performance. Of two management consultants promised, only one was made available. He, apart from his own work,

> spent time and effort in the fields of printing and standardization as well as in fending off, for two years, inquiries as to why we were not supplying technicians as promised in these fields.

Even so, "progress exceeded expectations." Not only was the DMO reorganized, but in the process there was created an organization and management "trained in RY in the native language which is receiving significant assignments [and] turning out highly acceptable work."

The assistance consisted of the training of nine participants in specific branches of supply and management, the introduction of simple improvements such as the training of typists "for the first time on a standard keyboard in the touch-typing method," better typewriter maintenance, the introduction of twenty-five pieces of locally produced material-handling equipment (all paid for by the DMO), the use of locally produced cardboard boxes instead of wooden crates to save shipping costs, the design of a new stock control system, and a more rational delegation of powers.

The existence of university-trained personnel, often with knowledge of a foreign language, in most key management positions was an important factor in the success of the program. These officers, though not trained in supply-management techniques, had the competence to administer a nationwide program, while they developed an understanding of American concepts through a decade of contact and a recognition, desire and acceptance of the need for technical assistance with the willingness to take action.

AGRICULTURE AND RESOURCE DEVELOPMENT

The cases related to agriculture tend to illustrate that agricultural aid requires parallel programs in other fields. To expect the increase of agricultural production implies, in most instances, that goods will be exchanged for the new products. Furthermore, tools, roads, credit, warehousing, and other goods and services are intimately related to agricultural improvement. Here we approach cultural or setting problems.

Two examples illustrate successful programs. The first is Range

Development in AI. The chosen agricultural divisions have approximately 125,000 square miles of grazing lands. These lands cannot be used for any form of agriculture but grazing. The agreement for assistance in range development was signed in 1954. By 1963 the initial project had been brought to a successful completion, and the results were "outstanding." A range of about 115,000 acres was selected for intensive development. The reasons for its selection were: (a) the entire range was government-owned, and it had received some range-rights protection since 1952; (b) it was typical of the major range lands in AI; and (c) its location made it a good demonstration and training area.

The United States provided the services of a range technician from 1955 to 1960 plus some commodity support. The government of AI provided a technical and administrative staff to participate in and supervise the project work. Livestock for weight gain trials was provided by local livestock owners.

Financial support was adequate on both sides, and no natural disasters occurred to destroy the effectiveness of the project. AI personnel attached to the project were associated with it for long periods of time and hence they could accumulate experience in addition to technical training.

Within five years the major objective of the project had been accomplished. Trials of reseeding arid and semi-arid lands and restoration of natural vegetation by mechanical treatment had been conducted. Climatic and ecological data were assembled, range and forage plants were collected and identified, and a Range *Forage Plant Manual* was compiled and printed. Considerable technical training had been imparted to the personnel, and the interest of the local livestock owners had been stimulated by the use of their livestock—so that improvements in the weight of animals benefited them directly.

By 1963 an over-all Range Development Scheme had been devised by the AI government, and funds had been allotted for five years. The reasons for the success of this project were the priority placed by the government on range development, the competence of the American technician, and continuity of tenure of his AI counterpart. The accessibility of this range to the other major range areas in AI, and the participation of local livestock owners made it a compact project with clearly-defined aims.

The second illustration of agricultural success is the Groundwater Investigations in the Desert of RA. In 1959, RA established the General Desert Development Authority (GDDA) to reclaim and develop desert areas. The GDDA charted a work program involving a study of water resources of the desert and soil analysis to determine what crops could be grown.

The GDDA asked UNESCO and the United States for technical assistance. The agreement with the United States was signed in FY 1960. UNESCO's contribution has been confined to reviewing the proposed project. The United States contributed mechanical engineers and aeronautical personnel and provided some commodity support.

The project suffered an initial delay of ten to twelve months because of staffing difficulties at the field level and the late arrival of equipment. But apart from this initial delay, progress in most parts of the project has been satisfactory. By 1963 the operating team could list a long series of accomplishments.

The principal reasons for success seem to have been the planning and priority placed by the RA government upon the development of a valley project. It was a compact and a purely technical project handled by engineers. The competence of U.S. personnel and the dedication of their RA counterparts was great. The project was ultimately based on a study by U.S. technicians which outlined not only the phases of the investigation but also clearly set forth the responsibilities of all agencies concerned.

The Hybrid Maize Project of UG was not as successful. Since 1947–48, maize has ranked fourth among the seven major food grains produced in UG. A research program to develop hybrids was started in 1940, but it languished since no effort was made to promote the two double cross-breeds that were evolved.

Requests for technical assistance were initiated by the provincial government in 1952. Full-scale participation by the United States began in 1955. Active participation by AID ceased in this project by the close of FY 1962.

During this period, the United States provided seed, transport and field implements, processing equipment, seed-treatment material and about nine and one-half man-years total for three technicians. UG provided the land and administrative and technical staff for the project.

The project was taken up at "the strong urging of the government of UG." And yet the series of difficulties which arose might have been prevented by the UG government. The lengthy (edited) extract from the project report is instructive.

The "Maize Program" has run into a series of problems. Some have been of a temporary nature while others seem to have become permanent. Problems of a more permanent nature will be considered in this discussion.

1. Land

a. Early in the conception of the program it was recognized that the maize program would require a limited amount of land on a permanent basis. In the summer of 1956 the provincial director of agriculture started proceedings to acquire a 1000-acre farm. In the fall of 1956, purchase of this farm was sanctioned and money appropriated by the government of UG. In 1958, the government cancelled the acquisition of the farm and the purchase was dropped, because the government could get the land at no cost by legislation. The government did not acquire the land. In the summer of 1957, proceedings were started to acquire other land. This land belonged to the government and was rented to cultivators. On the assurance that this land would be given to the maize section, ICA (AID's predecessor) made available funds for purchase of equipment for this farm. Action was stopped in 1959 on the orders of the Regional Commissioner. The equipment for this farm had already been purchased so it was put into storage.

b. . . .

c. . . .

d. In February, 1960, another farm was turned over to the Maize Section. This farm (956 acres) is government land and is in three dispersed plots. Two of the plots with a combined acreage of 400-plus acres were taken over by the Maize Section. Two hundred acres of the land now held by the Maize Section is of a tight, compacted soil not suitable for maize production. In addition, this land is not serviced by a canal, and the only water available comes from two tube-wells not located on the farm proper. In the past, arrangements were made to have 28 hours water per week from one well and 46 hours per week from the other. This is sufficient water for only 55 to 60 acres of maize. In 1960, 112 acres of maize were planted and the water decreased to a point where only 55 acres of maize could be brought to maturity, and even this was damaged by drought. The total production of 1961–62 was meager. Negotiations for the purchase of one of these wells was still under way at last query made. . . .

2. Buildings

The buildings program, particularly the drying and processing buildings, has lagged far behind the rest of the program. Under the project agreement the government of UG agreed to furnish buildings for the U.S.-financed equipment. The equipment was ordered as early as 1956–57, and all has arrived. It was only in the fall of 1960 that the building of the seed houses was sanctioned and tenders opened. The actual building was begun in early 1961.

3. Government-Grower Relationship

As early as 1958 the government assured the growers a premium for producing hybrid maize seed. Yet year in and year out the government failed to live up to its agreement on time. Some growers did not receive payment until a year or more had expired. And ultimately, the price they were paid was well below the market price for comparable quantities of seed. These farmers did not continue growing maize seed under such conditions.

It should be noted that difficulties arose despite the fact that UG is not particularly deficient in administrative personnel, and the American officials attached to the project appear to have been dedicated and competent. The principal reason for the failure of the project seems to have been the lack of interest on the part of the government of UG.

The Community Development Program of AK provides another example of small success. The program was launched in 1952, and focused attention on the lack of capable rural leadership. A Committee on Higher Education (1954–55) recommended the establishment of Rural Institutes which would be located in the countryside and would prepare students specifically for service in rural areas.

The Ford Foundation made a very substantial financial contribution. With this aid, the government of AK established ten experimental Rural Institutes in 1956. A project agreement with the United States was signed in 1957 for further technical assistance, so the U.S. government entered the picture officially only after the first ten institutes had been operating for several months.

By 1963 the number of institutes had increased, but each of them was "a small and weak rural college" rather than the ambitious Rural Institute that had originally been envisaged. The curriculum showed the influence of urban traditions: new instruction methods were not adopted; integration of teaching research and extension never came about; by and large the universities refused to accept graduates from these institutes for post-graduate work. Teacher-training remained a paper plan.

The government of AK failed to live up to its commitments. Expenditures for capital outlay and operation were much less than the original estimates because AK drastically cut down its financial contribution. The quality of the staff was less than satisfactory, and its turnover was high because of low pay and the absence of a chance for promotions within the institutes. U.S. technical assistance was too little and too late. A full-time technician arrived nearly four years after the institutes started. When the program was altered and requests were made for technicians in rural health and sanitation, American policies turned out to be unduly rigid.

CONCLUSION

The cases chosen are of interest because the nature of their characteristics provides instructive analogies for other likely situations and experiences. In brief, frustrations, successes, false starts, and the satisfying administration of technical assistance projects are often similar from one project to the next. Each case is not entirely *sui generis,* although each case does have some of its own particular characteristics.

The data of this chapter tends to show that in technical areas (e.g., aviation and printing) the conceptions of host and donor are often not at variance. In such nationally more traditional fields as education, agriculture, and personal services, however, the differing values and goals of host and donor tend to create administrative differences and difficulties. Solutions, when they come about, need not imply a great and drastic change of values of the host (or donor).

The diffusion of technical knowledge lies, in part, in defining the goal and adapting institutional operations to approach that goal. Before the question or questions relating to adaptability can be raised, questions relating to the goal must be settled.

The goal in the mind of the donor, assuming that there is a single well-defined goal, need not be the goal in the mind of the recipient. Realistically, a single goal is unlikely to exist in the mind of either the donor or recipient. Personal, institutional, project, and program considerations are neither entirely dependent on nor entirely unrelated to each other. This is true for both parties in the assistance transaction.

The means, whether they be technical, financial, or personal, are always significant in the program's success. Often, however, the cultural milieu is neutral, although it too may be a factor of help or hindrance.

A country may accept a project or sum of money because it feels it can improve its economic position, while, in truth, the project may not fit into the larger plans of the receiving country. It needs the money and it may need the good will of the donor more than it needs the particular project which the donor for some reason wants to supply. The rationality of the recipient may be exercised in accepting assistance for a purpose which is entirely unknown to the donor. Conversely, the donor may desire a certain project to be put into effect because of policy or even domestic politics, yet the policy or politics of the donor government may mean little to the recipient country.

One experience, touching to the author as a teacher, illustrates in oblique fashion the rational confusions which arise in the minds of technicians from developing societies. A Thai government technician, studying at Syracuse University, came to ask for academic advice. The author responded by inquiring what sort of help he needed, and his comment was something like this:

My Buddha teaches me that wisdom and the good life consist

in reducing my desires. Economic development, on the other hand, teaches me that the good life consists in developing desires and wants, so that my people will work for them. What ought a reasonable man to do?

The cases in this chapter are ones in which technical assistance comes about as the result of arrangements between host and donor respecting the improvement of some host government function. The cases have an interest of their own. They indicate the kinds of issues and problems which United States and host public administrators face. Often the problems are administrative, but often they lie more deeply in the goals and wants of the two governments.

The cases reported by persons skilled in the art of public administration again reveal the sharp and therefore narrow focus of the technician. The implications of the several projects are scarcely mentioned. The role of the demonstration effect, if any, of the impact on other institutions, of the changes generated—these and similar issues are not recorded. One has the feeling that within a narrow focus, successes and failures are recorded with a high degree of sophistication. The estimate of the effects of time and implication are lacking; yet these effects are at the core of the technical assistance exercise.

V. Technological Diffusion and the Economic System

Up to this point in the discussion we have followed two general lines of approach. First we offered the anthropological argument about cultural transfusion in its most general sense. The purpose was to provide something of a very broad frame of reference to fix the argument. The second approach was much more detailed. It was directed toward reporting and evaluating the views of practitioners who were concerned with technical assistance, which is a special case of cultural diffusion. These turned out to be on the whole, narrowly focused.

Given the frame and detail it is now necessary to adduce some kind of order to give meaning to the process. This implies that we seek some limited generalizations about technical assistance based upon the data, both concepts and records, which we have. To this and some additional concept creation and theorizing becomes necessary to relate the record (experience) to a conceptual framework. The immediate concern of the practitioners has to be expanded so that we can consider interrelations and connections in concept and practical implementation.

An economic system dealing as it does with securing, allocating, and using scarce resources and distributing the income produced is a complex of related social processes which, for convenience, we may call institutions. Technology, the *knowledge* of the art of using and developing means which are physical and organizational in nature in order to secure, fabricate, and distribute goods and services, is itself an institutional complex which binds the economic subsystem to the other social subsystems.

Technology, as we are using the concept, concerns the development of ways and means of performing an economic service, accomplishing such a service, and providing outlets for the abilities and natures of individuals in that service. In brief, technology is a means of supplying and structuring the physical and organizational basis of the economy. Technology links reflection and speculation about production and organization. It is thus a factor of production.

In Chapter I the ideas of two twentieth-century anthropologists were presented to describe the aspect of institutions as patterns of behavior among individuals. The behavioral patterns were seen to have a charter and legitimation based, in part, upon their functions. In our discussion we synthesized the role of the individual and of the behavior of the group into a single process in which the group behavior operates and constrains the individual, while the individual, under given circumstances, supplies new content or direction to the process of the legitimation of institutions. Our own concern was not with any generalized theory of institutions or cultural change, but with the more specific problem of the conditions of technical diffusion. The intervening discussions gave examples of the problem and the difficulties attending it.

We are now in a position to suggest some limited generalizations, somewhere between the details of the practitioners and the "big picture" of the anthropologists. The economic-technical process of our concern consists of ongoing social processes in an underdeveloped country which is being influenced by ideas of technology and organization introduced by technicians from abroad, specifically from the United States, usually under the governmental auspices of the AID. The introduction of the AID ideas and personalities may make the economic process more complex by introducing new values of social behavior which must be legitimated. If the introduced technology can be adapted to the skill and interests of those directly concerned, and if the government supplies resources and moral support, the problem of technical diffusion becomes minimal, little different than the introduction of technical ideas to a U.S. enterprise. The introduction of the new ideas and personalities does not constitute the Westernization of an indigenous culture but the utilization of some notions and techniques used in the West.

At this point, a *caveat* is in order. It is improper to consider the cultures, e.g., of India and the cities of Africa and South-East Asia, which are being changed and adapted as primitive or even highly and inflexibly traditional. The impact of the West, as well as of the Soviet Union and of the other developing societies, e.g., Israel,

Egypt, and Mexico, are in effect world-wide and have been persistent. There is novelty, change, and experiment everywhere. There also is persistence in any organized social process. The earmarks of an institutional system are precisely those characteristics, persistence, and change—persistence with respect to technique and goal, change with respect to the same two components.

Parsons and Smelser[1] have suggested that there are four essential dimensions or characteristics implicit in any institutional process, characteristics which must be operable if the process is to continue. The first is the *adaptive function,* that is, the capacity for change in an institution in its reactions to internal and external circumstances. The second is what one may call the *legitimating function* —the imperative of the process to be purposive as seen by the actors—to obtain some goal. The third dimension is the problem of *maintaining personnel integration,* or developing cooperating behavior among the actors of the system, the actors being either institutions or people. Finally, there is the dimension or characteristic of the *maintenance of the integrity of the (ongoing) value and procedural systems,* even while these are undergoing some changes. Thus, it is argued, adaptation, purposiveness, actor cooperation, and pattern maintenance, are the essentials of an ongoing social process.[2]

The major burden of an earlier discussion was the consideration of characteristics which technical experts believe their colleagues should have if they are to be effective in the process of technical diffusion. The points of view expressed were largely those of American technicians. The cases also exposed the necessary conditions for controlled change.

The technical actors in the development process possibly tended to underestimate the need, or at least proclivity, of institutions to maintain their latent patterns in order to control the tensions rising from the introduction of new ideas. On the whole, the effectiveness of the diffusion process, as seen by many of the respondents, was in the capacity of the American technicians and their indigenous counterparts to "get along" with each other and thus with the institutions in which they were operating. In other words, there

---

[1] Talcott Parsons and Neil J. Smelser, *Economy and Society* (London: Rutledge and Kegan, 1956), p. 19.

[2] *Ibid.,* pp. 18–46, 51.

was a tendency to treat personal (and personnel) adaptation as an index of goal attainment. The smoother the adaptability and the greater the cooperative integration, the more likely was the goal of technical diffusion to be gained. For the technicians, the first goal was cooperation among the actors, the second getting the job done.

The two goals were treated as interdependent, each implied the other. There is no reason to believe, however, that personal and personnel adaptability within the institution will, by themselves, assure technical diffusion (getting the job done). Indeed, the argument might very well be the other way around, that the adaptation of the technical process may often imply or even require some friction at the personnel level. This is merely an academic way of stating that one cannot make an omelet without breaking eggs. Effective social change may imply frustration and disharmony in certain circumstances, until a new set of values and behavior patterns evolve from the actors. The idea that a revolution eats its own children is a statement of such frustration.

The characteristics which Parsons and Smelser ascribe to all institutions are, to be sure, purely formal. In any specific case these terms—the goal priority, structure, the cooperative and integrative aspects of the factors in the system, the tendency toward the maintenance of latent patterns, and the management of tension—must be given specific values, i.e., empirical definitions.

The conditions of adaptation, for example, may be examined historically in the specific light of how adaptations in particular situations have occurred. Each of the dimensions in any specific case can, and for analytical purposes must, be specifically, i.e., historically, defined.

According to the respondents whose comments were discussed earlier, at least four factors from outside the technical diffusion process impinge on it. They are: (1) the general level of education, (2) the competence of the administrators, (3) the technical personnel reserve pool, and (4) the personalities of technicians. These factors affect institutions which are being adapted. Let us hasten to add that all the impinging forces are obviously more than the four we have mentioned. Again, in specific cases, unmentioned factors may be of crucial importance, but the four cited above are generally conceded by the respondents to be of major significance.

The administrator of a program of technical aid would perforce determine and isolate other impinging factors and probably would isolate institutional dimensions other than those discussed by Parsons and Smelser.

We have, nevertheless, a model which is useful in devising some generalizations about technological and technical diffusion.

The adaptation of an institution to new personalities and new techniques, in and of itself, does not assure the successful achievement of purpose nor the redirection of the institutional process toward a new purpose. Smoothness of operation and acceptability of new personnel does not assure the necessary and relevant adaptations of the process, including the goals of the process. The introductions of new technologies into an economic system might imply the creation of a new or modified economic and socio-psychological system, rather than the persistence of the essentials of the older system, with only slight modifications. Factories are not likely to succeed in rural, preliterate, mystical societies. Economic innovations which require linked or parallel adjustments and innovations cannot be introduced without generating changes of serious and basic nature throughout the society. Economic structure, politics, and social life generally may all be involved. Where a technical change is merely grafted on to an institution, however, the total effect may be negligible.

Each of the four autonomous factors affects the four dimensions of the process, but each in a special way depends upon the nature of the dimensions, the nature of the autonomous factors and the interactions between and among the dimensions which define the technical process. Thus, administrative competence may be sufficient to change the goals of the institutional process, but the fact of changing the goals may set up certain counteracting activities on the part of the pattern latency dimensions. A friction is created in the system then which requires solution by the actors. Personality characteristics then come into play, and the solution is sought in strengthening the adaptive power of the process, possibly through a heightened integration of all the actors concerned. The possibilities for interaction among the autonomous factors and the four dimensions are obviously very great and suggest that a process of technological diffusion is not likely to follow a unique, straight line of development, but a broad, and perhaps even poorly defined, winding path.

It should be constantly borne in mind that other autonomous factors affect the operation of a process. Such matters as budget availabilities, the priority systems instituted by the host and the donor governments, the availability of factors of production such as capital, labor, and management, the size of the markets and their structure; these and hundreds of other factors have a bearing on the success or failure of technical diffusion. On the whole, such factors may be considered as *data* in the administrative programing so far as the United States is concerned. The size and nature of the markets, the availability of capital and labor, and other such considerations cannot be controlled directly by the United States and probably cannot be controlled at all in the short run. Economic rather than technical assistance would more readily change the data of the system.

For our discussion, however, we may accept the economies as given and that personnel and ideas rather than goods, are the major U.S. contribution. Economic aid bears directly on production through capital advances, and includes the creation of markets and budgets. This leaves the personnel (training) consideration as the most significant factor, and possibly the easiest to manipulate.

From the point of view of personnel functions, that is, educational level, administrative capacity, technical pool of the host, and the U.S. personnel characteristics, the first three are, to a great extent, considered in the very selection of the program. In a short period the United States cannot do much to change the educational level of the host country, its administrative capacity, nor its technical pool. What it can vary is the donor personnel, since the United States can choose and train its own personnel with some discrimination. To a limited extent host personnel may be trained and chosen.

The problem of technical diffusion can be, in a very rough sense, simplified into two categories, (1) the choice of appropriate (U.S.) personnel in the light of the degree of adaptability of the system they are to improve, and (2) the capacity of the institutional process in the host to adjust to outside forces. Then, in terms of the persistence or fluidity of the adaptive mechanisms, goal-choosing mechanisms, actor-integrative mechanisms, and mechanisms of behavioral persistence, the donor (U.S.) can attempt to deal with such matters as education and administrative capacity and technical pool *through the choice and training of personnel,* including host personnel if possible.

What we have asserted does not solve the problem, but defines a condition of technical diffusion. All other autonomous factors may be assumed non-operative for the moment, and interest may be centered on four major adjustive factors and their reaction to personnel choices.

The latency principle is based on the observation that institutions in operation, or when subject to change, tend to exhibit signs of behavioral persistence. This persistence is often roundly damned by technicians who view their function as bringing improvement to the institutional operation. An operating institution which does not minimize its efforts to secure a given goal, for example, or which operates in order to secure less than a maximum effect, or actually works toward its own destruction, is considered imperfect, inefficient, dysfunctioning, or irrational, depending on the values of the observer. It is clear, however, that such criticism may be unwarranted and even wrong. The nub of the criticism is the allegation that the host actors do not know their own interests and are confused by ignorance, tradition, or general incompetence.

Yet if we assume, as do many sociologists and anthropologists, that institutions are purposive, one must test institutional latency in the light of purpose and effectiveness before criticizing the principle. If, in the economic jargon, one can show that the latency-persistence principle is rational, i.e., conserves resources and tends to maximize net yield given the actual environment of the institution, then latency is not equal to ignorance, sloth, indifference, or tradition, rather to the economic use of resources, including labor. Institutional latency, of course, may be improper in a different setting, say in the United States or in a changed host scene. But given the world in which the institution is operating, the presumption should be that the latency is rational.

One may suppose that its degree is related to the actor's belief that the behavior pattern, given the resources, is doing the job. If difficulties arise, this shifts the basis of cultural diffusion from the institution as the first target for improvement to the setting (resources and organization) with the institution becoming the second (reaction) target.

In one sense, then, the problem of technical diffusion is a problem of management. Management may be said to equal process plus objective plus human effort.[3] In other words, management, the control of an activity, may be viewed as equal to the process, which is the persistent behavior or latency of the institution, the objective or the goal choice, and the human effort, which is the cooperative or integrative consideration. Management is the adaptive mechanism in the sense that it attempts to control the latency, the goals and the human effort. From the over-all consideration of technological diffusion, management is the adaptive power or function of the ongoing social process. Therefore, the U.S. personnel and the other autonomous variables which are available should be directed towards the adaptive or managerial function. The control of the adaptive mechanisms implies a control over motives and sanctions (i.e., rewards, either positive or negative), rather than a direct attack on the latency of the institution. Of course the major managerial control is the host government itself. The strategy of development cannot be imposed as long as the host is not allowed to make its choices and govern!

THE POVERTY OF ECONOMICS IN THE ECONOMICS OF POVERTY

There seems to be no uniquely valid technique whereby culture is transmitted from a well-developed society to a less well-developed society. We do not have a full grasp about how values and the technical apparatus of a developed society become transformed in the very process of being diffused into another society. What we know is that progress implies some change within and without the institutions in question. In the Western World institutional interrelations are often taken for granted. The factory and the institutions of capital ownership, production, price determination, factory discipline, political organization, educational system, trade unions, and social security, to name only the obvious interrelated institutional structures, are fairly well understood by the actors as parts of a functioning whole. Yet, underdeveloped countries have

[3] John F. Mee, *Management Thought in a Dynamic Economy* (New York: New York University Press, 1963), p. 9.

either surrogate institutions for some of those mentioned, or in some instances only slightly developed institutional forms which carry out the functions or similar functions of the Western institutions cited above. It is therefore difficult and often impossible to prognosticate and anticipate institutional reactions and personal adjustment which are likely to ensue with the advent of, let us say, a factory or factory system.[4] Nurkse, at the end of his book on capital formation, suggested that these problems of institutional organization and reorganization are not within the purview of economics, so that sociology will have to take over.[5]

Practitioners of economics typically deal with the allocation of scarce resources with the objective of maximizing net returns. The resources are quantifiable, often tangible, and are available in markets; the outputs too, are mensurate in commonly understood units. Even when economists come up with alternative choices which lead to alternative solutions, the analysis tends to be tidy, and sometimes even determinate, within the constraints imposed by the definition of the problem. But when one is concerned with cultural diffusion or technical assistance, the universe of discourse —the constraints imposed by definition and experience—are not so clearly known and often are only vaguely apprehended by the analyst. Economic analysis tends, by its logic, to seek some kind of a position of equilibrium. Economic development, insofar as it uses the idea of technical assistance or technical diffusion, is dedicated in the first instance toward creating imbalances or disequilibriums in the system.[6] Even though the ultimate result of a disequilibrium

---

[4] From the theoretical viewpoint, our knowledge must be based on experience rather than on logic and assumption. But since our experience is limited, we tend to substitute either logic (such and such a relation is formally necessary) or experience drawn from other milieu. What is lacking is a knowledge of the social process of the particular place and subject of our concern. In a rapidly changing world this is most difficult, and we must rely on approximations of reality.

[5] Ragnar Nurkse, *Problems of Capital Formation in Underdeveloped Countries* (New York: Oxford University Press, 1953), p. 157. Nurkse gave such problems to sociology. But no matter who is academically responsible, the issues must be faced by anyone concerned with the practicality of cultural diffusion.

[6] This is not intended to revive the "balanced vs. unbalanced" growth argument. We are only asserting that social and economic change cannot occur simultaneously and in fixed proportions in a social system, so that it grows like a balloon being inflated.

situation might be some new equilibrium with higher levels of income, the interesting and relevant problem is the path of the induced disequilibrium to a new equilibrium or at least to some novel (hopefully stable) arrangement among the relevant social factors. The problem is complicated by the tendency for economic decisions to be irreversible. Once resources are allocated for use, they cannot be used again without incurring a loss.

Can we then define some generally accepted functions of technical aid, and so impose constraints within which the analysis will take place? As the analyses (or common sense and experience) require, additional variables may be introduced. This is not an unusual procedure in any behavioral analysis.[7]

ENDS AND MEANS

There is general agreement that the ideal of technical aid is to improve the per capita income of the recipients of such aid. This is a valid notion, and in the short run one could argue that the purpose of technical aid is to improve the per capita income and standard of life of the group which is directly aided.

Thus, technical aid to agriculture is designed, or should be, in the first instance to improve the status of the farmers receiving help and advice. But a moment's reflection indicates that this is a restricted point of view. Technical aid in agriculture is undertaken not only to benefit farmers but also for the general benefit of the society. The increase of the agricultural production is expected to help the urban dwellers too. Furthermore, the increase in food for the urban dweller is presumed to have beneficial effects on the production of the industrial sector. The interrelations and interconnections between the agricultural sector and the industrial sector are considerations which cannot be avoided because of their essential position in the whole exercise.

In economic theory the element of competition is a significant factor and operates in any market—the monopolistic, duopolistic, or oligopolistic—as long as some (marginal) resources are free to move from lesser to more effective and productive uses. The more

---

[7] The assumption of labor mobility, for example, is often withdrawn as the analysis of wages or labor income proceeds, to make the analysis "more realistic."

productive uses can afford to pay, and will pay, a generally higher price for the scarce factors. Variations in the nature and quality of output, changes in the relative quantities of factors going into a unit of a finished product, and other adjustments are competitive in their import.

No society has successfully or arbitrarily institutionalized all economic activity. This is true even where the government or some other institution plans a segment of the whole of the economic system. As experience indicates in the Soviet Union and elsewhere, where the price system is replaced by a "command" allocation of resources, fairly widespread unplanned activity occurs to supplement or frustrate the plan!

In both reality and in the economic analysis of the Western World, the role of the market as the allocator of scarce resources persists regardless of the degree of monopoly or public planning. Government planning and the role of monopoly, in fact, are not so great as to destroy the mobility of resources entirely. It may even be argued that planning, in part, substitutes a theoretically ideal market for the imperfect one at hand. Thus in a developed society, improving the lot of the farmers, or of any other particular group, may properly be assumed to have an effect on other sectors of the economy which supply or use the products of the benefited group. In brief, the interconnections in the Western World reach every segment of that society.

This is not valid as a generalization in underdeveloped countries. In some economies, Kenya, Thailand, Colombia, or Iraq, for widely spaced examples, possibly a quarter to half of the gross national product does not enter any market at all, and production and consumption are only vaguely related to money prices. Farmers tend to be subsistence farmers in many instances. Barter and communal responsibility often take the place of the money-price mechanism. Capital accumulation takes the form of inventories of consumer goods produced at home or luxuries, e.g., gold ornaments in India, rather than productive capital goods to be used in the process of creating new income. The offer of technical assistance to subsistence farmers, or to farmers whose conception of investment is the hoarding of gold ornaments, will clearly have different effects than similar technical assistance offered to farmers who think in terms of improving their stock, acquiring new tools, or securing education for their children. The setting in which technical assistance is offered becomes extremely important if one is to offer any comment on the technique of helping farmers.

With respect to resource allocation, the technical adviser first has to ask himself, "Are the people whom I am attempting to help using their resources inefficiently, given the nature of resources, the skill, and the setting in which the economic activity is taking place?" This question is important because a frequently implied *assumption* is that people in underdeveloped countries somehow are inefficient (irrational) in their use of the materials, skills, and land presently at their disposal. Then it would follow that by re-ordering available resources, more could be produced, more in terms of real income. Let us examine this argument from the standpoint of agriculture.

Agriculture may be taken as the crucial test of possible irrationality because in that industry, it is often argued, the extended family system, the communal village system, and sheer ignorance and inertia inhibit inventiveness and rational behavior. Disguised unemployment, often ascribed to agriculture, after all is the antithesis of unemployment resulting from a wage or money contract system. If industry and commerce are irrational in their behavior, and thus wasteful of resources, the irrationality and waste must be relatively *greater* in agriculture. Stated in another way, the market system and Western technology are more apparent in industry and trade than in farming. Therefore, if the notion of economic irrationality in agriculture is successfully questioned, the denial becomes even stronger for urban economic activity.

Professor Theodore W. Schultz[8] takes exception to the commonly held view that factor allocation in underdeveloped countries is faulty from the viewpoint of maximizing net returns. He cites an imposing empirical literature, one striking quotation being from an unpublished doctoral dissertation of Dr. David Hopper.[9] Hop-

[8] *Transforming Traditional Agriculture* (New Haven: Yale University Press, 1964), pp. 36ff., 71ff.

[9] Cited in Schultz in his unpublished Ph.D. thesis, "The Economic Organization in the Village of North Central India," presented at Cornell University, June, 1957. "An observer in Senapur cannot help but be impressed with the way the village uses its physical resources. The age-old techniques have been refined and sharpened by countless years of experience, and each generation seems to have had its experimenters who have added a bit here

per's thesis deals with the town of Senapur, India, where he lived for a while, studying the life of the community.

Professor Schultz first attacks the question of whether farmers in underdeveloped countries habitually practice a poorly derived allocation of resources by a forthright criticism of the prevailing doctrine that disguised unemployment is a mark of agriculture in impoverished societies.

There are three prongs to Schultz's attack on what he considers a conventional but erroneous assumption, one frequently based on Professor P. N. Rosenstein-Rodan's assumption that about 25 per cent of the agricultural labor force in Eastern and Southeastern Europe is totally or partially unemployed.[10]

The second prong of the Schultz attack is to substitute for the assumption of zero marginal productivity of labor in traditional agriculture the empirical findings which tend to refute this notion. He refers to the writings of Oshima and Buck.[11] Incidentally, the criticism that what appears to be disguised unemployment in underdeveloped countries may be the attachment of labor to agriculture, and is related to peak requirements, has been used as a gentle corrective to the more or less accepted view of general overabundance of labor in agriculture.[12]

The third prong of Schultz's argument is a direct empirical examination of output and employment in Indian agriculture dur-

and changed the practice there, and thus improved the community lore. Rotations, tillage and cultivation practices, seed rates, irrigation techniques and the ability of the blacksmith and potter to work under handicaps of little power and inferior materials, all attest to a cultural heritage that is richly endowed with empirical wisdom. To the question 'Are the people of Senapur realizing the full economic potential of their physical resources?' . . . the answer must be 'yes,' for in general, each man comes close to doing the best he can with his knowledge and cultural background." *Ibid.*, p. 45.

[10] P. N. Rosenstein-Rodan, "Problems of Industrialization of Eastern and Southeastern Europe," *Economic Journal* (1943), 53. "Economic Development with Unlimited Supplies of Labour," *The Manchester School* (May, 1954), pp. 141–42. Cf. W. Arthur Lewis.

[11] Harry T. Oshima, "Underemployment in Backward Economies: An Empirical Comment," *Journal of Political Economy* (June, 1958); and John Lossing Buck, *Land Utilization in China* (Chicago: University of Chicago Press, 1937), I, 7.

[12] Gerald M. Meier, *Leading Issues in Development Economics* (New York: Oxford University Press, 1964), p. 79. Meier cites Professor J. Viner as indicating a confusion between seasonal and disguised unemployment.

ing and after the 1918–19 influenza epidemic. The mortality rate in this epidemic in India was amazingly large, somewhere in the neighborhood of twenty million people, or about 6 per cent of the 1918 population.[13]

The data show that for all of British India, acreage sown in crops (in millions of acres) decreased from 265 in 1916–17, to 255 in 1919–20. Schultz estimates the labor coefficient to be .349 and also uses some sample surveys of India estimated for more recent years.[14] Given a labor coefficient of .4, the 1919–20 output should, according to Schultz's calculation, have equaled 96.7 per cent of the 1916–17 number of acres sown to crops. Actually, the observed result is 96.2 per cent. This remarkably close relation tends to support Schultz's contention.[15]

To be sure, Schultz's observations apply entirely to the India of nearly fifty years ago, but the argument is sufficiently persuasive to cast a deep doubt first on the notion that the marginal productivity of labor in agriculture approaches zero, and second, that traditional agriculture has little or no flexibility in the reallocation of inputs to secure maximum output. Flexibility exercised permits rational choices.[16] He argues that reproducible, nonhuman capital tends to be much larger as an investment input in underdeveloped areas than is generally believed.[17]

[13] Schultz, *op. cit.*, p. 64ff.

[14] *Ibid.*, p. 67. The labor coefficient of .4 means that a decrease of employed labor in agriculture by 10 per cent, holding the other inputs constant, would result in a 4 per cent reduction in agricultural output (acreage sown, in this case). This is quite in accord with Schultz's estimates based upon the 1916–20 data.

[15] *Ibid.*, p. 83ff.

[16] *Ibid.*, p. 97ff. See also "Surplus, Agriculture and Development: Facts and Theories," Morton Paglin, *American Economic Review* (September, 1965), p. 815ff. Professor Paglin, after analyzing data from Farm Management Studies, finds that the data does not support the zero marginal productivity of labor and disguised the unemployment argument. "The position of Schultz is fully borne out by the present study." Paglin also refers to "Surplus Labor in Greek Agriculture, 1953–1960," A. A. Pepelasis and P. A. Yotopoulos, Center of Economic Research Monograph Series Two, Athens, 1962. Paglin argues that improving the health and technology of farm workers would improve output. This is our argument that improving the setting is a condition of growth.

[17] *Ibid.*, p. 97ff.

In Punjab, India, Schultz estimates that about 53 per cent of the value inputs were in reproducible nonhuman capital, 13 per cent in land, and 34 per cent in labor. For the United States, the estimates are 55 per cent for reproducible nonhuman capital, 12 per cent for land, and 33 per cent for labor.

His conclusion is that additional investment in land, i.e., net new investments in reproducible nonhuman capital, tends to be *not* worthwhile because of the generally low economic level of the impoverished societies. In other words, new investments in the land would not be so fruitful as investments made elsewhere, unless the price of agricultural commodities rose in relation to other prices, or more correctly, to the returns of capital invested in other nonagricultural activities, either at home or abroad.

The rationality of investment in agriculture, which is after all the key to the measure of viability and adjustability of agriculture to market considerations, is supported by additional information. From a study done on agriculture in Kenya, it appears clear that the Kenya (African) farmers do tend to allocate their effort and investments in the anticipation of prospective yields. The decisions of farmers tend pretty much to follow a pattern which is explicable in terms of prices. The author concludes in part that:

> Within the wide range of land-labor ratios considered, it is most profitable to produce two cash crops in the coffee/tea and pyrethrum/tea ecological zones. Only in the pyrethrum/coffee zone is it more profitable to grow only one crop—in this case, coffee.[18]

Professor Stanley Diamond finds that rationality, given the modalities of primitive society, is a functioning principle. He writes:

> ... so far as I know, no primitive economic system is dysfunctional with the available technology. Neither does it use technology in a wasteful or inefficient way, no matter what "bizarre" means are brought into play to dispose of surplus

[18] Eric Clayton, *Economic Planning in Peasant Agriculture* (Ashford, Kent: Wye College [University of London], 1963), p. viii. The present writer is also impressed by similar comments by his own foreign graduate students, some of them government officials on leave from their native lands, and others preparing for academic or public service careers.

beyond the point where the subsistence needs of the group are met, or to stimulate exchange.[19]

The major reason that low level agriculture appears to be so rigid, however, is that the *opportunities* for adjustment are on the whole very slight because the *setting* of the agriculture industry is rigid, and thus provides few alternatives to the farmer. The uncertainties of politics imply the wisdom of hoarding money and goods; lack of markets restrict innovation and product variation; poor roads and the scarcity of consumer and producer goods put a damper on inventiveness; knowledge is lacking and so on.

Bauer and Yamey argue in this general way,[20] basing their contention largely on British West African experience. In addition to showing that the particular economic undertakings are limited by market size and capital supply, they also assert that the economic activity undertaken by urban and rural groups is varied, and consciously directed toward income. In the Bauer and Yamey discussion, as in the U.N. Report on "Land Reform,"[21] one gets the impression that the setting, the whole structure of economic (and social) life is being exploited, but the economic potential of the setting is low, at best. This is not to argue that ideal changes in the social structure or capital supply automatically would result in great increases in social well being, but that knowledge and technique, too, are necessary resources. Improvements in knowledge and technique, by themselves, may very well be ineffective, unless and until they are functionally linked to appropriate economic factors.

The notion of competition involves the adjustability and viability of the setting of any particular economic activity. This includes not only the availability of capital but an availability of knowledge and skill (human capital) consistent with the new setting. One may conclude therefore that a major function of technical assistance is

[19] Stanley Diamond, "The Search for the Primitive," *Man's Image in Medicine and Anthropology* (New York: Columbia University Press, 1963), pp. 86–87.

[20] P. T. Bauer and B. S. Yamey, "Economic Progress and Occupational Distribution," *Economic Journal* (December, 1951), reprinted in *Readings on Economic Development,* T. Morgan, G. W. Betz, N. K. Choudhry, eds. (Belmont, Calif.: Wadsworth Publishing Co., 1963), p. 286ff.

[21] *Land Reform—Defects in Agrarian Structure and Obstacles to Economic Development* (U.N., 1951), reprinted in *Readings, op. cit.,* p. 208ff.

to loosen the institutional framework which surrounds agriculture (or industry) by simultaneously supplying capital, new ideas, and new markets for the increased output. An increased supply of agricultural products will not, in and of itself, create its own demand; but the supply of other goods wanted by farmers must increase.

It can be shown, for example, that tribes living in more favorable environments, or having complex technologies, or with relatively extensive human resources, produce more goods and have more to show for the labor of their members in the way of further production and of permanent structures than other peoples who live in less favorable settings, or whose technical equipments are simpler, or whose populations are smaller.[22]

If our contention is correct, then the approximate ideal of maximization of yield of agriculture is often being met insofar as the individual farmer is concerned. But the ideal is being realized in a social system with a very low level of per capita income, even when the resources are being used about as effectively as they can be. In other words, rationality obtains, but the system's limitations are such that rationality produces a low income. Improving the agricultural situation may trigger changes in the other sectors, so that the benefits of change will multiply. As we pointed out earlier in the discussion, the choice of agriculture was made as an example because that industry is often assumed to be the least economically rational. Industry and commerce are more related to the usual rationality which marks Western business activity. Furthermore, disguised unemployment is peculiar to family or communal farming and is unrelated as an institutional device to activities using wage contracts.

Yet there is the possibility that what appears to be economic irrationality in farming is really the rational use of inferior resources, plus a powerful imperative of the setting of agriculture.

Some Guides to Development

The assumption that technical assistance and the technician can improve the situation merely by suggesting the reorganization or

[22] Melville J. Herskovits, *Economic Anthropology* (New York: Knopf, 1953), p. 308.

reorientation of existing resources, including human knowledge, seems doomed almost before it is applied. To be sure, increases in the use of fertilizer in the form of a demonstration will increase production in a given crop year, but such increases are neither likely to be continued nor adopted by other farmers unless it proves to be profitable. The solution rather lies in improving the economic status of agriculture, which includes, of course, improving the viability and responsiveness of the setting in which agriculture finds itself.

In agriculture, technical assistance might profitably orient itself in the area of linkage of the agricultural institutions to the total setting. Questions regarding the effects of an improvement in organization, skill, knowledge, and specific capital in agriculture on the (political and) economic market become relevant.

Considerations of ideology and rationality which have intrigued so many writers and students in the field of development seem to have been overemphasized as a hurdle. The thread running through this chapter, and indeed the entire study, is that the managers of productive activity in the underdeveloped countries are rational, but rational within the constraints of the system in which they are operating.

If it were possible to improve the gross output of agriculture, thereby raising the per capita output of agriculture, without changing any other aspect of the society, the results might very well be disastrous for farmers. Cheaper food would lower the money wage in the city, through reduced agricultural prices. If, as is likely to be the case, the price elasticity of demand for agricultural products is less than unity, the real income, i.e., the urban goods and services which farmers could buy would likely fall with the improved agricultural output. Even if prices of manufactured goods fell, it is not likely they would fall in relation to farm prices. Benefits would accrue less to the farmers than to the urban folk. Farmers would possibly be in a position to eat more, if they were producing food which could be consumed at home, but their claims on non-farm-produced income would not improve much, or at all. The result might be an impetus to village industry or barter, but these are not the roads to development. Education, capital accumulation, and general welfare on the farm would not be improved in this manner.

On the other hand, the employers of labor in the city might be in a position to enjoy the profits of increased agriculture through lower prices, but this improvement would be of short duration because the farmers would not continue to grow more than could be profitably sold. This would lower urban real wages. A distressed labor income situation due to lowered real wages in urban areas surely would not invite (wage goods) investments except possibly for export goods.

If, however, the improvement of agricultural output were associated with positive changes in the social setting by autonomous activity, e.g., in actions supportive of private and public investments through the decisions of a planning body or the market, more agricultural output might lead to a reduction in labor costs to urban manufacturers and producers, and to more investment. It is immediately suggested that public services—schools, medical care, flood control, mobile markets, adult education, and electricity, to name a few—would be of inestimable value in improving the status of the farmer as he improves the status of the urban areas.

No exact formula for relating agricultural growth to industrial growth can be given in the abstract. However, a general conceptual statement may have some value. For improvement in agriculture to be persistent it should be related to the increased availability of nonagricultural goods and services. In the short run, the importance of consumer goods and the provision of services needed and wanted by farmers seems indicated. For a longer period, the improvement in manufacturing output and in the institutions of transport and exchange on a continuing basis seem indicated. Credit policies, subsidies, and incentives are among the mechanisms available. Considerations of ownership and rights of tenants, taxes, and educational availabilities are also involved.

Markets seem to be the major impediment to agricultural improvement, and technical assistance to agriculture is fruitless if the market cannot absorb the added output at a reasonable price. The role of imports in providing exchange goods for improved agriculture at the onset of improvement should never be overlooked.

One question arising from this discussion concerns how a planning body of the host or the donor country can induce a disequilibrial situation, or to use a synonym, an unbalanced growth situation, in a social system. The purpose would be to arrange linkages between agriculture and the industrial and political settings to shift the supply and demand for goods to higher levels. Economic theory has always argued that capital is necessary for such a dynamic readjustment. In recent years the notion of capital has been extended to include human capital, that is, human education and knowledge, to give one a wider choice of behavior based upon his own capacities. In addition to such capital and human improvements, organizational structures and the legitimating of new social processes are required. The new social processes must be legitimated if they are to be persistent. Otherwise, the new processes will be but a demonstration project which will close down once the technical aid is withdrawn.

As is always the case in social change, the key to change is people, not people as individuals, but people operating in an institutional framework, overcoming obstacles, setting new goals, and applying imaginative, novel measures to create a new set of constraints upon behavior, consistent with higher incomes. The conclusion implies that additional capital and consumer goods (as originally guessed by many economists) are necessary if not sufficient conditions to support economic growth.

Final Remarks

The diffusion of technology, in which we should include social organizations which have a direct or important indirect affect on economic development, is not usually a traumatic experience. The underdeveloped countries have, in the main, had a long and deep experience with Western ways, and often have reacted so as to adapt the ways of the West to their own situations. A major difference between the ways of the West and those of the emerging societies is found in agriculture. The primacy of agriculture as an economic factor can scarcely be overestimated. The fact that more than half the world is always hungry, and subsists on a meager diet which itself is frequently threatened, is proof enough of the importance of agriculture.

To concentrate only on specific projects is not meaningful as a developmental device, because successful projects, by themselves, offer no clue to their total interconnected effects. To go to the other extreme to attempt a total plan is also not meaningful because the total set of interrelations and effects cannot be known beforehand. Besides, the donor is simply not in the position to exercise more than a pointed influence on the host. The pragmatic approach is through the limited vehicle of examining the institutional frame and its setting and operation, then adjusting the frame to the setting and *vice versa,* so that interconnections and links are made, while the institutional dimensions are adjusted to the goals.

Index